BRANCHES OF GOVERNMENT

READING COMPREHENSION

TRUE OR FALSE

After reading about the **U.S. Constitution**, read each statement below and determine if it is true or false. If the statement is true, color the coin that corresponds with that question. If the statement is false, cross out that coin value. When you are finished, add the TOTAL of **ALL TRUE** coin values to reveal a 4-digit code. One digit of the code has been provided for you. If the total is 625, a 6 would go in the first box, the 2 in the second box and so on.

A 75 | B 25 | C 50 | D 100 | E 100 | F 75 | G 50 | H 25

A. The Preamble begins with the words "We the people."
B. The United States had a document before the Constitution called the Bill of Rights.
C. Article III is the Executive Branch, and it is responsible for creating the laws.
D. The U.S. Constitution is a document that states how the federal government should operate.
E. The opening part or introduction of the Constitution is called the Resolution.
F. The 19th Amendment gave women the right to vote.
G. George Washington became known as the "Father of the Constitution."
H. The Constitution, or plan of government, is organized into ten different parts called Articles.

After shading the coins based on your answer, add the value of ALL TRUE statements to get the final total. Record your answer in the boxes below.

☐ ☐ ☐ 2

MYSTERY WORD

After reading about the **Branches of Government**, determine if each statement below is true or false. Color or shade the boxes of the **TRUE** statements. Next, unscramble the mystery word using the large letters of the **TRUE** statements.

U.S. citizens vote for both the president and vice president on election day in November. **D**	The Judicial Branch, Article III, is the federal court system. **E**	Congress can override a presidential veto with a ½ vote. **F**	The Constitutional Convention took place in Boston. **M**
The Legislative Branch can declare war. **T**	Appeals Courts have three judges and do not use a jury. **S**	To impeach means to set aside the punishment for a federal crime. **U**	The main job of the Executive Branch is to interpret the laws. **A**
Each branch has a different purpose and function. **I**	Once the Supreme Court makes a decision, the decision is final. **R**	Together, both the Senate and the House of Representatives are called Congress. **P**	The president is also the Commander-in-Chief of the military. **N**
The president can appoint Supreme Court judges with consent of the Senate. **E**	The Senate has two hundred members and is referred to as the "Lower House." **V**	Supreme Court justices serve a twelve-year term. **B**	Under the Supreme Court are the thirty-six Court of Appeals. **C**

Unscramble the word using the large bold letters of only the **TRUE** statements.

MULTIPLE CHOICE

After reading about **Checks and Balances**, answer each multiple-choice question below. Then, count the number of times you used each letter as an answer (ABCD) to reveal a 4-digit code. Letters may be used more than once or not at all. If a letter option is not used, put a zero in that box.

1. What vote is needed in the Senate to ratify a treaty?
A. One-fourth
B. One-half
C. Two-thirds
D. Three-fourths

2. What is the main job of the Legislative Branch?
A. Create the laws
B. Enforce the laws
C. Interpret the laws
D. Veto the laws

3. Which Supreme Court case established judicial review?
A. Bush v Gore
B. Tinker v Des Moines
C. Marbury v. Madison
D. Miranda v Arizona

4. Which of the following is part of the Executive Branch?
A. Cabinet
B. Vice President
C. President
D. All of the above

5. Which part of government must approve of presidential appointments?
A. Senate
B. Vice President
C. House of Representatives
D. Chief Justice

6. The first successful congressional override occurred under which president?
A. John Tyler
B. George Washington
C. John F. Kennedy
D. Franklin D. Roosevelt

7. How many houses is Congress composed of?
A. Two
B. Four
C. Six
D. Eight

8. When was the Constitutional Convention?
A. 1776
B. 1781
C. 1785
D. 1787

Count how many times you used each letter as a correct answer (ABCD) to determine the 4-digit code. Record your answer in the boxes below.

# of A's ☐ # of B's ☐ # of C's ☐ # of D's ☐

MYSTERY MATCH

After reading about the **Senate**, draw a line from the left-hand column to make a match in the right-hand column. Your line should go through **ONE** letter. When you complete all the matches, use the letters with a line THROUGH them to unscramble a mystery word. You MUST start and end your line at the **arrow points**.

Filibuster	Number of Senate members
Convicted	Vice president's job in the Senate
Upper House	Strategy of prolonging a new bill from passing
100	First meeting of Congress
Six years	Declared guilty
Break a tie	Synonym for laws
Legislation	Nickname of the Senate
New York City	Term length of a senator

Letters: J F I E E B S F V O R T P R G H D

Unscramble the 8 letters to reveal a mystery word:

DOUBLE PUZZLE

After reading about the **House of Representatives**, determine the word that corresponds with the statements provided below. Spell the corresponding word in the boxes to the right. You may or may not use all squares provided for each answer. Any numerical answers must be spelled out. Next, use the numbers **under** indicated letters to reveal a secret word.

1. Last name of the first Black American elected to the House (6)
2. The leader of the House is called the ____ of the House (1)
3. The representatives are redistributed in each state every ____ years (7)
4. The states are divided into ____ (2)
5. The House of Representatives is also known as the "____ House" (5)
6. An accurate count of the population required by the Constitution
7. Number of years for the term length of a representative (3)
8. Representatives must have lived in the U.S. for ____ years (8)
9. Last name of the first woman to serve as Speaker of the House
10. Synonym for constituents in the state in which they live (4)

SECRET WORD 1 2 3 4 5 6 7 8

PARAGRAPH CODE

After reading about the **White House**, head back to the reading and number ALL the paragraphs in the reading passage. Then, read each statement below and determine which paragraph **NUMBER** the statement can be found in. Paragraph numbers MAY be used more than one time or not at all. Follow the directions below to reveal the 4-digit code.

A. First Lady Dolley Madison, wife of President James Madison, famously saved a portrait of George Washington before fleeing.
B. The White House sits on eighteen acres of beautifully landscaped grounds, including the South Lawn and the Rose Garden.
C. It also contains the State Dining Room, Blue Room, and Red Room, which are used for official events.
D. The building has a swimming pool, bowling alley, and a movie theater.
E. Construction of the White House began in 1792, after President George Washington selected the site.
F. The East Wing contains the offices of the First Lady and is often used for hosting tours and events.
G. In 1891, President Benjamin Harrison had electricity added to the house for the first time.
H. Originally, the building was called the "President's Palace" or "Executive Mansion."

ELIMINATE ALL EVEN-NUMBERED paragraphs that you used as an answer. Record the remaining numbers (in the SAME order in which you recorded them above) in the boxes below.

SECRET CODES & MYSTERY WORDS

By Lisa Fink

Contact the author :
Lisa@ThinkTankTeacher.com

TABLE OF CONTENTS

ABOUT THIS WORKBOOK

History doesn't have to be boring — especially when it comes with a dash of mystery and a twist of F-U-N, including secret codes and mystery words! This collection of 24 reading comprehension passages is designed to spark curiosity and make history come alive for kids ages 10+ (or grades 5-8).

WHAT'S INSIDE?

23 Reading Passages: (2 full pages each)

Each passage is crafted to draw your kids into the past, making history relatable and intriguing for learners at home or in the classroom. To ensure understanding, each reading comprehension passage comes with two interactive worksheets.

Worksheet 1: Crack the 4-Digit Code!

This activity turns reading into a puzzle, keeping kids motivated to dive deeper into the material. Your learners will answer comprehension questions based on the passage and correct answers will reveal a secret 4-digit code. Programmable locks aren't required, but they can take the fun to the next level!

Worksheet 2: Mystery Word!

To ensure they've truly grasped the material, kids answer another set of questions, based on the same reading passage, that unveil a secret word.

WHY IT WORKS:

Active Engagement: By turning reading comprehension into a game, kids are more likely to stay engaged, motivated to learn and eager to finish the task. Game-based learning requires active participation. Rather than passively reading and answering questions, kids are actively seeking answers to solve the puzzle.

Encourages Critical Thinking: Game elements often require kids to think critically and make connections between different pieces of information. To find the correct answers and solve the puzzle, they must analyze the text carefully, improving their comprehension skills.

Reinforcement Through Fun: The excitement of uncovering codes and secret words reinforces key historical concepts in a way that sticks. Kids may be more willing to go back and re-read sections of the passage to ensure they have the correct answers.

Incentive to Learn: The reward of discovering a secret code or mystery word acts as a powerful incentive. Kids are more likely to pay close attention to details in the reading passage, knowing that each answer brings them closer to solving the puzzle. This can lead to a deeper understanding of the content.

Increased Motivation: When an assignment includes elements like secret codes or mystery words, it feels less like work and more like a fun challenge. This added layer of excitement motivates kids to complete the task to "win" or uncover the hidden element.

Versatile Use: These activities are perfect for homeschooling or classrooms — use as part of your daily lessons, supplemental homework, or independent study.

Promotes Positive Reinforcement: Successfully uncovering a secret code or mystery word provides immediate positive feedback, which reinforces the learning experience. This sense of achievement boosts confidence and encourages kids to tackle future activities with enthusiasm.

HOW TO FIND THE MYSTERY WORD

There are three different types of mystery word activities.

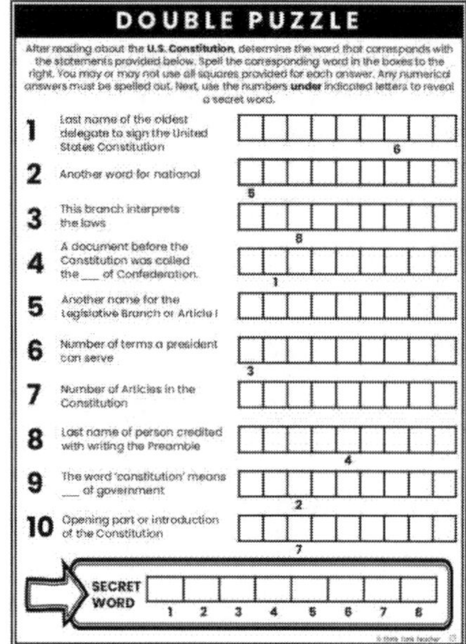

DOUBLE PUZZLE

After reading about the **U.S. Constitution**, determine the word that corresponds with the statements provided below. Spell the corresponding word in the boxes to the right. You may or may not use all squares provided for each answer. Any numerical answers must be spelled out. Next, use the numbers **under** indicated letters to reveal a secret word.

1 Last name of the oldest delegate to sign the United States Constitution

2 Another word for national

3 This branch interprets the laws

4 A document before the Constitution was called the ___ of Confederation.

5 Another name for the Legislative Branch or Article I

6 Number of terms a president can serve

7 Number of Articles in the Constitution

8 Last name of person credited with writing the Preamble

9 The word 'constitution' means ___ of government

10 Opening part or introduction of the Constitution

SECRET WORD 1 2 3 4 5 6 7 8

DOUBLE PUZZLE

After reading the passage, determine the correct word that corresponds with statements 1-10. Spell the corresponding word in the boxes to the right. You may or may not use all squares provided for each answer. Any numerical answers **must** be spelled out. Next, use the numbers **under** indicated letters to reveal a secret word.

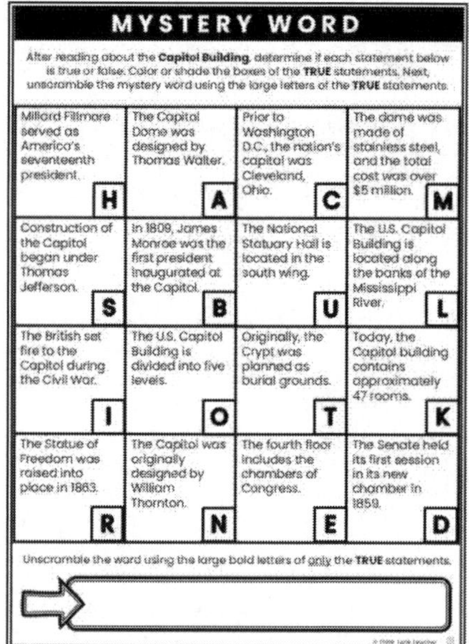

MYSTERY WORD

After reading about the **Capitol Building**, determine if each statement below is true or false. Color or shade the boxes of the **TRUE** statements. Next, unscramble the mystery word using the large letters of the **TRUE** statements.

Millard Fillmore served as America's seventeenth president. H	The Capitol Dome was designed by Thomas Walter. A	Prior to Washington D.C., the nation's capitol was Cleveland, Ohio. C	The dome was made of stainless steel, and the total cost was over $5 million. M
Construction of the Capitol began under Thomas Jefferson. S	In 1809, James Monroe was the first president inaugurated at the Capitol. B	The National Statuary Hall is located in the south wing. U	The U.S. Capitol Building is located along the banks of the Mississippi River. L
The British set fire to the Capitol during the Civil War. I	The U.S. Capitol Building is divided into five levels. O	Originally, the Crypt was planned as burial grounds. T	Today, the Capitol building contains approximately 47 rooms. K
The Statue of Freedom was raised into place in 1863. R	The Capitol was originally designed by William Thornton. N	The fourth floor includes the chambers of Congress. E	The Senate held its first session in its new chamber in 1859. D

Unscramble the word using the large bold letters of only the **TRUE** statements.

MYSTERY WORD

After reading the passage, determine if each statement is true or false. Color or shade the boxes of the **TRUE** statements. After all TRUE answers have been shaded, unscramble the mystery word using the large, bold letters of only the TRUE statements.

MYSTERY MATCH

After reading about **Checks and Balances**, draw a line from the left-hand column to make a match in the right-hand column. Your line should go through **ONE** letter. When you complete all the matches, use the letters with a line THROUGH them to unscramble a mystery word. You MUST start and end your line at the **arrow points.**

Judicial Branch	One-sided
Treaty	A formal agreement between countries
Impeach	Term of Supreme Court appointments
Unilateral	Accused of misconduct while in office
Declare War	Interprets the laws
Life	Power of Congress
Article II	Baron de Montesquieu
French philosopher	Executive Branch

Unscramble the 8 letters to reveal a mystery word:

MYSTERY MATCH

After reading the passage, draw a line from the left-hand column to make a match in the right-hand column. Your line should go THROUGH **one** letter. When you complete all the matches, use the letters with a line THROUGH them to unscramble a mystery word. You MUST start and end your line at the arrow points. Then, unscramble the 8 letters to reveal the mystery word. **IMPORTANT: Your line MUST start with an arrow TIP on the left and end at an arrow TIP on the right.** If you do not draw from arrow tip to arrow tip, you will not be able to reveal the hidden word.

HOW TO FIND THE SECRET CODE

There are three different types of secret code activities.

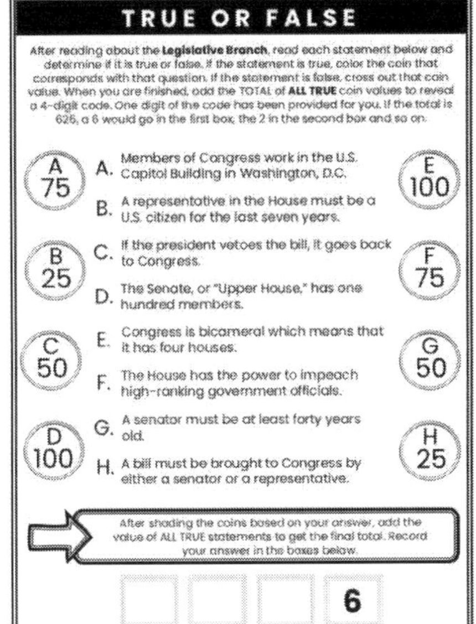

TRUE OR FALSE

After reading about the **Legislative Branch**, read each statement below and determine if it is true or false. If the statement is true, color the coin that corresponds with that question. If the statement is false, cross out that coin value. When you are finished, add the TOTAL of **ALL TRUE** coin values to reveal a 4-digit code. One digit of the code has been provided for you. If the total is 626, a 6 would go in the first box, the 2 in the second box and so on.

Coin	Statement	Coin
A 75	A. Members of Congress work in the U.S. Capitol Building in Washington, D.C.	E 100
	B. A representative in the House must be a U.S. citizen for the last seven years.	
B 25	C. If the president vetoes the bill, it goes back to Congress.	F 75
	D. The Senate, or "Upper House," has one hundred members.	
C 50	E. Congress is bicameral which means that it has four houses.	G 50
	F. The House has the power to impeach high-ranking government officials.	
D 100	G. A senator must be at least forty years old.	H 25
	H. A bill must be brought to Congress by either a senator or a representative.	

After shading the coins based on your answer, add the value of ALL TRUE statements to get the final total. Record your answer in the boxes below.

			6

TRUE OR FALSE

After reading the passage, determine if each statement is true or false. If the statement is true, color, circle, or shade-in the coin that corresponds with that question. If the statement is false, cross out that coin value. When you are finished, add the **TOTAL** of **ALL TRUE** coin values to reveal a 4-digit code. If you are working on statement D, be sure you find the coin that is labeled D. The final number of the code will always be provided for you.

PARAGRAPH CODE

After reading the passage, number **ALL** the paragraphs. Then, read each statement and determine which paragraph **NUMBER** the statement can be found in. Paragraph numbers MAY be used more than one time or not at all. When all paragraph numbers have been found, **ELIMINATE ALL EVEN-NUMBERED** paragraphs that you used as an answer. Record the remaining numbers (in the SAME order in which you recorded them) in the boxes at the bottom. **Example: 85362147 = 5317 (after crossing off all EVEN numbers, the remaining numbers in the order in which they were found is 5317)**

PARAGRAPH CODE

After reading about the **Capitol Building**, head back to the reading and number ALL the paragraphs in the reading passage. Then, read each statement below and determine which paragraph **NUMBER** the statement can be found in. Paragraph numbers MAY be used more than one time or not at all. Follow the directions below to reveal the 4-digit code.

- **A** During the Civil War, construction of the Capitol Building was stalled.
- **B** The Statue of Freedom sits atop the dome, symbolizing liberty, and raised into place in 1863.
- **C** Construction of the building began under George Washington, with the cornerstone laid (first stone of the foundation) in 1793.
- **D** This hall was called the 'Old Hall of the House' from 1809–1857.
- **E** The House of Representatives held its first session in the new chamber in 1857.
- **F** The Crypt includes thirteen statues to represent the thirteen colonies.
- **G** Architecturally, it combines neoclassical elements derived from ancient Greece and Roman temples.
- **H** The most iconic feature is the Capitol Dome, designed by Thomas Walter.

ELIMINATE ALL EVEN-NUMBERED paragraphs that you used as an answer. Record the remaining numbers (in the SAME order in which you recorded them above) in the boxes below.

MULTIPLE CHOICE

After reading about the **Powers of Congress**, answer each multiple-choice question below. Then, count the number of times you used each letter as an answer (ABCD) to reveal a 4-digit code. Letters may be used more than once or not at all. If a letter option is not used, put a zero in that box.

1. How many representatives in the House does each state have?
   A. Two
   B. Six
   C. Twenty
   D. Depends on the population
2. Where do all tax and spending bills begin?
   A. Senate
   B. House of Representatives
   C. Supreme Court
   D. Rules Committee
3. What leader of the Senate is responsible for breaking a tie?
   A. Speaker of the House
   B. Vice president
   C. Secretary of State
   D. Commander-in-chief
4. Who will choose the vice president if there is no majority in the Electoral College?
   A. President
   B. Senate
   C. Supreme Court
   D. House of Representatives
5. Which of the following is NOT a power of Congress?
   A. Establish post offices
   B. Admit new states to the Union
   C. Veto laws
   D. Create lower federal courts
6. What branch of government is the U.S. Congress a part of?
   A. Legislative Branch
   B. Executive Branch
   C. Judicial Branch
   D. Parliament Branch
7. What are federal taxes used to pay for?
   A. National defense
   B. Roads
   C. Schools
   D. All of the above
8. Which of the following is NOT a power of Congress?
   A. Regulate and control trade
   B. Determine if laws are constitutional
   C. Create immigration laws
   D. Declare war

Count how many times you used each letter as a correct answer (ABCD) to determine the 4-digit code. Record your answer in the boxes below.

# of A's	# of B's	# of C's	# of D's

MULTIPLE CHOICE

After reading the passage, answer each multiple-choice question. Then, count how many times you used each letter as a correct answer (ABCD) to determine the 4-digit code. Letters may be used more than once or not at all. If a letter option is not used, put a zero in that box. **Example: B,C,C,D,C,A,A,C = 2141** (The A was chosen as a correct answer for 2 questions, the B was chosen 1 time, C was used 4 times and D was chosen as a correct answer 1 time)

FOUNDATIONS OF GOVERNMENT

U.S. CONSTITUTION

The U.S. Constitution is a document that states how the federal government should operate. It outlines what the federal government can do, as well as what the federal (national) government cannot do. The Constitution outlines the three branches of government. Then, it discusses the purpose of each branch in detail. The Constitution also includes basic rights for all Americans.

The Constitution is organized into three main sections: the preamble, articles, and amendments. The U.S. Constitution is the highest authority in the nation and the oldest government document that is still in use today. The Constitution, or plan of government, is further organized into seven different parts called Articles. These include Legislative Powers, Executive Powers, Judicial Powers, States' Powers and Limits, Amendments, Federal Powers, and Ratification.

The United States had a document before the Constitution called the Articles of Confederation. The Articles of Confederation had many major problems, flaws, or weaknesses. The Articles of Confederation did not allow the government to collect money. In turn, this meant that the government did not have any money to operate.

The Constitutional Convention

In 1787, the weaknesses of the Articles of Confederation were discussed at the Constitutional Convention in Philadelphia. Here, the Constitution was drafted to replace the Articles of Confederation. At the Convention, the writers decided that the government needed three branches to operate. The three branches created a balance of power within the federal government. Each branch had a clear purpose, but none could become too powerful. This was particularly important to Americans at the time as they had just broken away from the tight rule of the British government.

The Framers of the Constitution created a "living" document, which means that it can be changed at any given time. James Madison became known as the "Father of the Constitution."

Article I of the Constitution is the Legislative Branch, also known as Congress. This branch makes the laws. Article II is the Executive Branch, and it is responsible for enforcing the laws. The Judicial Branch, or Article III, interprets the laws. The Constitution created a system of federal government that could operate without impacting the basic rights of any of the citizens.

Structure and Framework

The opening part or introduction of the Constitution is called the Preamble. The Preamble was written by some of the most educated men in America at the time, and it outlined basic rights for all Americans. It made sure that the power was with the citizens, not with a government. The Preamble is primarily a summary of how the government can operate and how the citizens will be treated. Gouverneur Morris is credited with writing the famous Preamble that begins with the words "We the people."

The Constitution also has amendments. An amendment means that there can be a change or addition to the Constitution, if needed. The first ten amendments came in the late 1700's, known as the Bill of Rights. The Bill of Rights protects certain freedoms of the citizens. It clearly states that citizens have the right to freedom of speech, religion, assembly, press, and the right to a fair trial, among others.

Other amendments include the 13th Amendment which abolished slavery, the 19th Amendment which gave women the right to vote and the 22nd Amendment which limits the number of times a person can be elected as President of the United States to two terms.

Thirty-nine of the fifty-five delegates who attended the Convention signed the new document. Many of those who refused to sign did so because the new plan of government did not originally contain a Bill of Rights. After nine of thirteen states ratified, or approved, the document, the signing of the Constitution occurred on September 17, 1787. Benjamin Franklin was the oldest delegate to sign the United States Constitution. Thomas Jefferson and John Adams did not attend the Convention because they were serving as diplomats outside of the U.S. at that time.

Principles

The Constitution consists of seven principles, such as Separation of Powers, which provide the foundations for the American government. The purpose of the principles (foundation for a system of beliefs) was to help create an effective government that would guard against tyranny.

The Constitution is the most important document in the history of the United States. Before the Constitution, each of the states operated like individual countries. There was not a strong federal government to hold them all together. There was not even a president to represent the United States. The Constitution created a federal government that allowed the states to operate together, as well as partly on their own.

TRUE OR FALSE

After reading about the **U.S. Constitution**, read each statement below and determine if it is true or false. If the statement is true, color the coin that corresponds with that question. If the statement is false, cross out that coin value. When you are finished, add the TOTAL of **ALL TRUE** coin values to reveal a 4-digit code. One digit of the code has been provided for you. If the total is 625, a 6 would go in the first box, the 2 in the second box and so on.

B 25

A. The Preamble begins with the words "We the people."

B. The United States had a document before the Constitution called the Bill of Rights.

C. Article III is the Executive Branch, and it is responsible for creating the laws.

D. The U.S. Constitution is a document that states how the federal government should operate.

E. The opening part or introduction of the Constitution is called the Resolution.

F. The 19th Amendment gave women the right to vote.

G. George Washington became known as the "Father of the Constitution."

H. The Constitution, or plan of government, is organized into ten different parts called Articles.

After shading the coins based on your answer, add the value of ALL TRUE statements to get the final total. Record your answer in the boxes below.

2

DOUBLE PUZZLE

After reading about the **U.S. Constitution**, determine the word that corresponds with the statements provided below. Spell the corresponding word in the boxes to the right. You may or may not use all squares provided for each answer. Any numerical answers must be spelled out. Next, use the numbers **under** indicated letters to reveal a secret word.

	Statement	Boxes (9)	Number under box
1	Last name of the oldest delegate to sign the United States Constitution		6 (box 7)
2	Another word for national		5 (box 1)
3	This branch interprets the laws		8 (box 3)
4	A document before the Constitution was called the ___ of Confederation.		1 (box 2)
5	Another name for the Legislative Branch or Article I		
6	Number of terms a president can serve		3 (box 1)
7	Number of Articles in the Constitution		
8	Last name of person credited with writing the Preamble		4 (box 5)
9	The word 'constitution' means ___ of government		2 (box 3)
10	Opening part or introduction of the Constitution		7 (box 3)

SECRET WORD

1	2	3	4	5	6	7	8

BRANCHES OF GOVERNMENT

The Founding Fathers were responsible for the start of the United States. Their focus at the Constitutional Convention in Philadelphia was on a government with limited power that guaranteed liberties (freedoms) to the citizens.

There are three different sections of government in the United States. These different sections are referred to as branches. Each branch has a different purpose and function. The branches work together in many forms, but the power of each branch is separated from the powers of the other branches. This is to prevent one branch of government from becoming too powerful and is known as checks and balances. The three branches of government are the Legislative, Executive, and Judicial. The role of each branch is outlined in the U.S. Constitution in Articles I, II, and III.

The three branches must work together to make sure the government operates successfully. With the separation of powers, no branch can infringe on the rights of the people. All three branches are headquartered in either the Capitol Building (Congress), the White House (President) or the Supreme Court (Justices) in Washington, D.C.

The Legislative Branch

The Legislative Branch, Article I, includes the Senate and the House of Representatives. It is considered bicameral, which means it has two houses or parts. Together, both the Senate and the House of Representatives are called Congress. The main purpose of this branch is to write or create bills that become laws.

The Legislative Branch can restrict the power of the president, if needed. If the president vetoes, or rejects, a bill, Congress can override it with ⅔ vote and make it a law. The Legislative Branch also has non-legislative (non-lawmaking) powers. This branch can declare war, impeach the president, confirm or reject treaties, propose amendments and approve or deny the president's appointments.

The citizens of the United States vote for Senators and Representatives to represent them in Congress. The Senate has one hundred members and is referred to as the "Upper House." Each state has two Senators who represent the interests of that particular state in the Senate. The House of Representatives has four-hundred-thirty-five members and is referred to as the "Lower House." The number of representatives of each state is based on the population.

The Executive Branch

The Executive Branch, Article II, includes the President of the United States. The president is the leader of this branch with the title Head of State. The Executive Branch also includes the vice president, and a group of advisors called the cabinet. The citizens of the United States vote for both the president and vice president on election day in November. The main job of the Executive Branch is to enforce the laws. Presidents may serve two terms. Each term is four years. The Constitution outlines three requirements for presidential candidates.

The members of the cabinet are appointed (chosen) by the president, then voted on in Congress. The cabinet helps the president make informed decisions across a variety of issues, including military operations. The cabinet includes fifteen different departments such as the Department of Education and Department of Energy.

The president can appoint Supreme Court judges with consent (approval) of the Senate, make treaties, and pardon federal offenders. To pardon someone means to set aside the punishment for a federal crime. The president is also the Commander-in-Chief of the military. Many mistakenly believe that the president can declare war but only Congress has that power.

The Judicial Branch

The Judicial Branch, Article III, is the federal court system. The main job of this branch is to interpret the laws. The Supreme Court is the highest court. It can decide if the laws passed by Congress are legal and follow the Constitution. It can declare acts by Congress and the president illegal and unconstitutional. It can also hear cases from lower courts that have been challenged. These cases come to the Judicial Branch for final review. Once the Supreme Court makes a decision, the decision is final.

Under the Supreme Court are the thirteen Court of Appeals or Appellate Circuit Courts. Appeals Courts have three judges and do not use a jury. Under the Court of Appeals, there are 94 District Courts. District Courts hear civil and criminal trials, with one judge and a jury.

The judges on the Supreme Court are called justices, with the leading judge called Chief Justice. At any given time, the Supreme Court has nine justices. Many of these justices stay on the Supreme Court for life. Members of the Judicial Branch are appointed by the president, then confirmed (approved) by the Senate.

PARAGRAPH CODE

After reading about the **Branches of Government**, head back to the reading and number ALL the paragraphs in the reading passage. Then, read each statement below and determine which paragraph **NUMBER** the statement can be found in. Paragraph numbers MAY be used more than one time or not at all. Follow the directions below to reveal the 4-digit code.

A The Legislative Branch also has non-legislative (non-lawmaking) powers.

B The cabinet helps the president make informed decisions across a variety of issues, including military operations.

C Many mistakenly believe that the president can declare war but only Congress has that power.

D The Executive Branch also includes the vice president, and a group of advisors called the cabinet.

E It can declare acts by Congress and the president illegal and unconstitutional.

F The role of each branch is outlined in the U.S. Constitution in Articles I, II, and III.

G The House of Representatives has four-hundred-thirty-five members and is referred to as the "Lower House."

H With the separation of powers, no branch can infringe on the rights of the people.

ELIMINATE ALL EVEN-NUMBERED paragraphs that you used as an answer. Record the remaining numbers (in the SAME order in which you recorded them above) in the boxes below.

MYSTERY WORD

After reading about the **Branches of Government**, determine if each statement below is true or false. Color or shade the boxes of the **TRUE** statements. Next, unscramble the mystery word using the large letters of the **TRUE** statements.

U.S. citizens vote for both the president and vice president on election day in November. **D**	The Judicial Branch, Article III, is the federal court system. **E**	Congress can override a presidential veto with a ½ vote. **F**	The Constitutional Convention took place in Boston. **M**
The Legislative Branch can declare war. **T**	Appeals Courts have three judges and do not use a jury. **S**	To impeach means to set aside the punishment for a federal crime. **U**	The main job of the Executive Branch is to interpret the laws. **A**
Each branch has a different purpose and function. **I**	Once the Supreme Court makes a decision, the decision is final. **R**	Together, both the Senate and the House of Representatives are called Congress. **P**	The president is also the Commander-in-Chief of the military. **N**
The president can appoint Supreme Court judges with consent of the Senate. **E**	The Senate has two hundred members and is referred to as the "Lower House." **V**	Supreme Court justices serve a twelve-year term. **B**	Under the Supreme Court are the thirty-six Court of Appeals. **C**

Unscramble the word using the large bold letters of only the **TRUE** statements.

CHECKS AND BALANCES

The Constitution is the supreme law of the land in the United States, written in 1787 at the Constitutional Convention in Philadelphia. The word constitution simply means 'plan of government'. The U.S. Constitution establishes the rules and laws of the government and sets basic rights for its citizens. The U.S. Constitution is the oldest constitution still in use today and many nations have modeled their government after that of the United States.

The U.S. government has three main branches that function together as well as separately. Each branch has their own powers to act on behalf of the government and to limit the power of the other branches. The Framers of the Constitution made sure that no one branch of government could have too much power, creating a system known as "checks and balances."

The Influence of Montesquieu

Influenced by the French philosopher Baron de Montesquieu, the Framers divided the government into three branches, creating a separation of powers. The Legislative Branch, or Article I, makes the laws and is also known as Congress. Congress is made up of two houses, the Senate and the House of Representatives. The Executive Branch, or Article II, enforces the laws. The Executive Branch includes the president, vice president, and cabinet members who advise the president. The Judicial Branch, or Article III, interprets the laws. The highest federal court in the United States is the Supreme Court. Montesquieu also believed these bodies were subject to the rule of law, meaning no one is above the law, not even the president.

Checks and balances are essential to ensure that one branch of government doesn't have too much power over the others. By limiting powers and requiring cooperation among these branches, the Framers of the Constitution designed a government that could prevent tyranny and promote justice. For example, the president (head of the Executive Branch) is the Commander-in-Chief of the armed forces. This means the president has the power to direct military operations. However, this authority is checked by Congress, part of the Legislative Branch, which has the power to declare war and approve funding for military operations. Without the approval of Congress, the military cannot be fully deployed or sustained financially, ensuring that the president does not have unilateral (one-sided) power over military decisions.

Another significant check on executive power is the president's authority to make treaties with other nations. A treaty is a formal agreement between countries. The president can negotiate agreements and alliances, but for those treaties to be valid, they must be ratified (approved) by a two-thirds majority in the Senate. This requirement prevents the president from engaging in foreign diplomacy that may not have broad support from elected representatives, thus ensuring that the nation's foreign policy reflects a collective decision.

Appointments and Impeachment Powers

The president nominates federal officials such as cabinet members and those who work in the Federal Reserve, but the Senate (Legislative Branch) must approve those people. The president also has power over the Judicial Branch by appointing (choosing) judges during their time as president if any vacancies should come up. However, Congress can impeach both members of the Executive and Judicial branches. If a president is impeached (accused of misconduct while in office), the Chief Justice of the Supreme Court presides over the trial in the Senate where the 100 U.S. Senators serve as the jury. Supreme Court appointments are for life, which allows the president to influence the judiciary long after leaving office. However, these appointments require Senate approval, adding a layer of oversight.

Within Congress, the two houses keep the Legislative Branch balanced. The House of Representatives and the Senate check each other when new laws are being created. Both houses must approve the law in identical form before it is enacted.

Vetoes and Overrides

The president can "check" Congress by vetoing (rejecting) a bill. Congress then has the ability to override the veto with a two-thirds majority vote. The Supreme Court can decide if laws approved by the Legislative Branch or Presidential Orders are constitutional or unconstitutional. This process, known as judicial review, was established in the landmark Supreme Court case of Marbury v. Madison in 1803. Congress can also check the Judicial Branch by proposing amendments to the Constitution, which can override judicial decisions.

The first successful congressional override occurred under President John Tyler in 1845. Franklin D. Roosevelt vetoed 635 bills, more than any other president. Of those, only 9 were overridden by Congress. A congressional override is very rare.

MYSTERY MATCH

After reading about **Checks and Balances**, draw a line from the left-hand column to make a match in the right-hand column. Your line should go through **ONE** letter. When you complete all the matches, use the letters with a line THROUGH them to unscramble a mystery word. You MUST start and end your line at the **arrow points**.

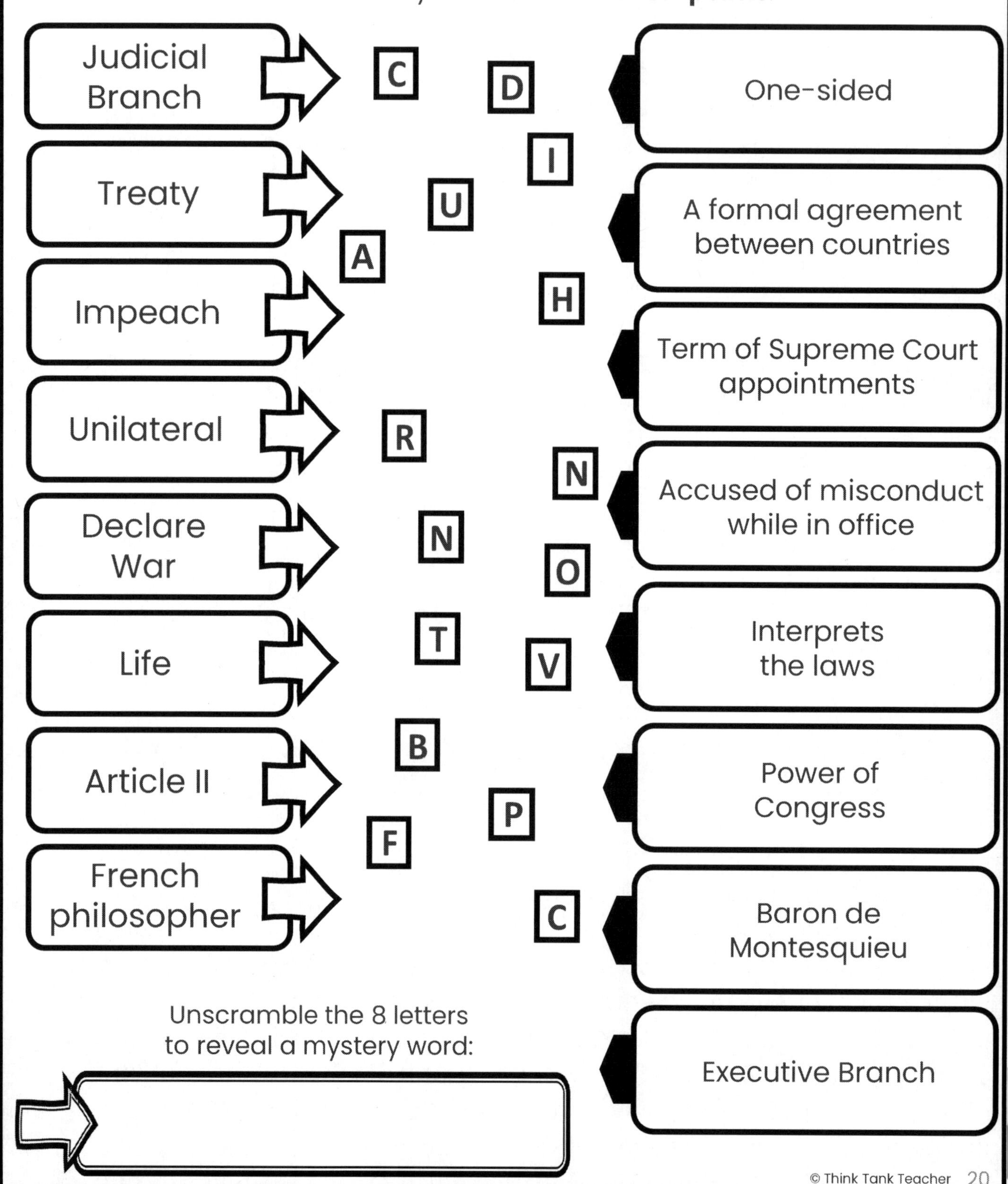

Judicial Branch
Treaty
Impeach
Unilateral
Declare War
Life
Article II
French philosopher
C
D
I
U
A
H
R
N
N
O
T
V
B
P
F
C
One-sided
A formal agreement between countries
Term of Supreme Court appointments
Accused of misconduct while in office
Interprets the laws
Power of Congress
Baron de Montesquieu
Executive Branch

Unscramble the 8 letters to reveal a mystery word:

MULTIPLE CHOICE

After reading about **Checks and Balances**, answer each multiple-choice question below. Then, count the number of times you used each letter as an answer (ABCD) to reveal a 4-digit code. Letters may be used more than once or not at all. If a letter option is not used, put a zero in that box.

1 What vote is needed in the Senate to ratify a treaty?

A. One-fourth
B. One-half
C. Two-thirds
D. Three-fourths

2 What is the main job of the Legislative Branch?

A. Create the laws
B. Enforce the laws
C. Interpret the laws
D. Veto the laws

3 Which Supreme Court case established judicial review?

A. Bush v. Gore
B. Tinker v. Des Moines
C. Marbury v. Madison
D. Miranda v. Arizona

4 Which of the following is part of the Executive Branch?

A. Cabinet
B. Vice President
C. President
D. All of the above

5 Which part of government must approve of presidential appointments?

A. Senate
B. Vice President
C. House of Representatives
D. Chief Justice

6 The first successful congressional override occurred under which president?

A. John Tyler
B. George Washington
C. John F. Kennedy
D. Franklin D. Roosevelt

7 How many houses is Congress composed of?

A. Two
B. Four
C. Six
D. Eight

8 When was the Constitutional Convention?

A. 1776
B. 1781
C. 1785
D. 1787

Count how many times you used each letter as a correct answer (ABCD) to determine the 4-digit code. Record your answer in the boxes below.

# of A's	# of B's	# of C's	# of D's

ARTICLE I

LEGISLATIVE BRANCH

The Legislative Branch, or Article I of the U.S. Constitution, is part of the federal (national) government of the United States. The main role of this branch is to create laws, although it has other responsibilities as well. The power of the federal government is divided between the three branches to have a separation of powers. This means that each branch has a different role and responsibility ensuring that the federal government operates without becoming excessively powerful.

The Legislative Branch is also known as Congress. Congress is bicameral which means that it has two houses: the Senate and the House of Representatives. The people who make the laws are called legislators. Members of Congress work in the U.S. Capitol Building in Washington, D.C.

The longest Article in the Constitution is Article I and it discusses the Legislative Branch in detail. While the Legislative Branch is only one of the three branches, it proves a vital role in ensuring the federal government's operation. The Legislative Branch helps to ensure that citizens get fair laws. The Legislative Branch also ensures that the other branches of government are operating smoothly.

Members and Leaders

The Senate, or "Upper House," has one hundred members with each state having two senators. The House of Representatives, or "Lower House," has four hundred thirty-five members but the number of representatives per state is based on population. The leader of the Senate is the vice president, but when they are not breaking a tie, the leader is called the President Pro Tempore. The leader of the House is the Speaker of the House.

Qualifications and Terms

There are different qualifications for each house outlined in Article I. A senator must be at least thirty years old. They must be a U.S. citizen for at least nine years and live in the state they represent. A representative must be twenty-five years old and a U.S. citizen for the last seven years. They must live in the state that they hope to represent.

Senators serve a six-year term. The senator can serve as many terms as they like because there is no term limit, as long as they are re-elected. Every two years, an election for senators is held. In this election, only one-third of the senators will be voted on. This means that the elections are staggered for the Senate. Representatives serve a two-year term. There are also no term limits in the House, as long as they are re-elected.

Legislative Process

The Legislative Branch helps make sure that the laws of the federal government are fair and just. An idea for a law, called a bill, must go through many steps called the Legislative Process. A bill must be brought to Congress by either a senator or a representative. The bill is then placed in a box called a hopper, given a bill number, and formally recorded. Next, the bill is introduced to Congress.

The bill would be assigned to a committee that is familiar with what the new bill is proposing (suggesting). For example, if the new bill involves roads, then it would go to the Transportation Committee. The bill is later debated by the House of Representatives and the Senate. The majority of one house has to vote for and approve the bill, then it goes to the other house for ratification (approval). The bill must get approval in identical form in both houses. If both houses vote on the bill and it gets approved, then it goes to the president.

The president can either sign the bill into law or veto (reject) it. If the president vetoes the bill, it goes back to Congress where they can override the veto with a two-thirds vote. This is all part of checks and balances.

Additional Powers

While the main focus of the Legislative Branch is drafting and passing new legislation (laws), it also has non-legislative (non-lawmaking) powers. Congress can declare war on another country or territory. There are often long debates before Congress declares war. Congress also negotiates treaties with other countries, when needed. Treaties require a two-thirds vote by the Senate.

Congress has the task of creating a budget from which the government operates. This budget is reviewed each year in depth. Congress can levy (collect) taxes and makes sure those taxes are being spent in the way that they should be spent.

Members of the Senate can approve high-level positions such as a Supreme Court Justice and the members of the president's cabinet. This is an important check on the power of the Executive Branch.

The House has extra tasks in addition to making new laws as well. For example, all tax bills have to start in the House of Representatives. The House also has the power to impeach high-ranking government officials. To impeach means to accuse of misconduct while in office.

TRUE OR FALSE

After reading about the **Legislative Branch**, read each statement below and determine if it is true or false. If the statement is true, color the coin that corresponds with that question. If the statement is false, cross out that coin value. When you are finished, add the TOTAL of **ALL TRUE** coin values to reveal a 4-digit code. One digit of the code has been provided for you. If the total is 625, a 6 would go in the first box, the 2 in the second box and so on.

A. Members of Congress work in the U.S. Capitol Building in Washington, D.C.

B. A representative in the House must be a U.S. citizen for the last seven years.

C. If the president vetoes the bill, it goes back to Congress.

D. The Senate, or "Upper House," has one hundred members.

E. Congress is bicameral which means that it has four houses.

F. The House has the power to impeach high-ranking government officials.

G. A senator must be at least forty years old.

H. A bill must be brought to Congress by either a senator or a representative.

After shading the coins based on your answer, add the value of ALL TRUE statements to get the final total. Record your answer in the boxes below.

6

DOUBLE PUZZLE

After reading about the **Legislative Branch**, determine the word that corresponds with the statements provided below. Spell the corresponding word in the boxes to the right. You may or may not use all squares provided for each answer. Any numerical answers must be spelled out. Next, use the numbers **under** indicated letters to reveal a secret word.

#	Statement	Letter boxes (9)	Secret-word number under box
1	The bill must get approval in ___ form in both houses		8 (box 8)
2	Minimum age of a senator		7 (box 4)
3	The bill is placed in a box called a ___		6 (box 5)
4	Another word for levy		9 (box 3)
5	To accuse of misconduct while in office		5 (box 2)
6	Number of years that senators must be a U.S. citizen for		2 (box 2)
7	Members of Congress work in the U.S. ___ Building		3 (box 1)
8	An idea for a law		1 (box 1)
9	The leader of the House is the ___ of the House		4 (box 4)
10	Number of years served for one term as senator		

SECRET WORD

1	2	3	4	5	6	7	8	9

CAPITOL BUILDING

The U.S. Capitol Building, along the banks of the Potomac River, is an iconic symbol of American democracy and home to the Legislative Branch of government. Located in Washington, D.C., it was designed by William Thornton and construction began in 1793. The original building has expanded over time, including the addition of its famous dome in the 1850s. Architecturally, it combines neoclassical elements derived from ancient Greece and Roman temples. Today, the Capitol Building is home to two chambers: the House of Representatives and the Senate.

History and Early Development

The U.S. Capitol was chosen as the seat of the U.S. government in 1790 under the Residence Act, establishing Washington, D.C., as the nation's capital. Prior to this, the nation's capital was Philadelphia, Pennsylvania. Construction of the building began under George Washington, with the cornerstone laid (first stone of the foundation) in 1793. However, it took decades to complete, with interruptions due to factors such as the War of 1812, when the British set fire to the Capitol in 1814. The building was eventually restored and expanded, reflecting the growing needs of the nation.

For several decades after the federal government moved to Washington, D.C., the Capitol served not only for legislative (law-making) functions but also as a site for Sunday religious services. These services were non-denominational and open to the public, reflecting the Capitol's multifunctional use during its early years. This practice of holding religious services in the Capitol continued well into the 19th century, with prominent figures like Thomas Jefferson, members of Congress and local citizens, regularly attending.

During the Civil War, construction of the Capitol Building was stalled. During this time, the building served as a hospital to treat wounded soldiers, military barracks (camps) and even a bakery to provide food and bread to Union troops.

Architectural Design

William Thornton's original plan was later enhanced (improved) by other architects, including Benjamin Latrobe and Charles Bulfinch, adding intricate details, and expanding the building. The most iconic feature is the Capitol Dome, designed by Thomas Walter. President Millard Fillmore,

America's thirteenth president, appointed Walter as the main architect to build extensions to the Capitol. Construction of the dome began in the 1850s and was completed in 1866. The dome was made of cast-iron, and the total cost was $1,047,291. The Statue of Freedom sits atop the dome, symbolizing liberty, and raised into place in 1863.

Inside the Capitol, the Rotunda and National Statuary Hall showcase artwork depicting key moments in American history. In the 1850s, two large wings were added to accommodate the growing number of lawmakers: the Senate Wing to the north and the House of Representatives Wing to the south. Today, the building contains approximately 540 rooms.

The Rotunda is a large, circular room beneath the Capitol Dome. It is used for ceremonial events and houses important artwork, including frescoes (murals) and statues that depict significant moments in U.S. history. The historical paintings are oil-on-canvas and measure twelve by eighteen feet, four of which feature scenes from the Revolutionary War.

The National Statuary Hall is located in the south wing and originally served as the meeting place for the House of Representatives. This hall was called the 'Old Hall of the House' from 1809-1857. The chamber floor is covered with alternating black and white marble tiles.

The U.S. Capitol Building is divided into five levels. The ground floor is mostly composed of committee rooms for congressional officers. Visitors on this level can tour the Hall of Columns, the Brumidi Corridors, the Old Supreme Court Chamber, and the Crypt. The Crypt was originally planned as the burial grounds for George and Martha Washington. However, their graves remain at Mount Vernon. The Crypt includes thirteen statues to represent the thirteen colonies. The second floor includes the chambers of Congress. The third floor includes gallery access to watch proceedings (meetings) when Congress is in session. The basement and the fourth floor include offices, machinery, and support for staff members.

Famous Firsts

Over its long history, the U.S. Capitol has been the site of significant events. In 1801, Thomas Jefferson was the first president inaugurated at the Capitol. It has hosted numerous State of the Union addresses, presidential inaugurations, and speeches that shaped American history. The building was also witness to the passage of landmark legislation, such as the Civil Rights Act of 1964. The House of Representatives held its first session in the new chamber in 1857. The Senate held its first session in its new chamber in 1859.

PARAGRAPH CODE

After reading about the **Capitol Building**, head back to the reading and number ALL the paragraphs in the reading passage. Then, read each statement below and determine which paragraph **NUMBER** the statement can be found in. Paragraph numbers MAY be used more than one time or not at all. Follow the directions below to reveal the 4-digit code.

A During the Civil War, construction of the Capitol Building was stalled.

B The Statue of Freedom sits atop the dome, symbolizing liberty, and raised into place in 1863.

C Construction of the building began under George Washington, with the cornerstone laid (first stone of the foundation) in 1793.

D This hall was called the 'Old Hall of the House' from 1809-1857.

E The House of Representatives held its first session in the new chamber in 1857.

F The Crypt includes thirteen statues to represent the thirteen colonies.

G Architecturally, it combines neoclassical elements derived from ancient Greece and Roman temples.

H The most iconic feature is the Capitol Dome, designed by Thomas Walter.

ELIMINATE ALL EVEN-NUMBERED paragraphs that you used as an answer. Record the remaining numbers (in the SAME order in which you recorded them above) in the boxes below.

MYSTERY WORD

After reading about the **Capitol Building**, determine if each statement below is true or false. Color or shade the boxes of the **TRUE** statements. Next, unscramble the mystery word using the large letters of the **TRUE** statements.

Millard Fillmore served as America's seventeenth president. **H**	The Capitol Dome was designed by Thomas Walter. **A**	Prior to Washington D.C., the nation's capital was Cleveland, Ohio. **C**	The dome was made of stainless steel, and the total cost was over $5 million. **M**
Construction of the Capitol began under Thomas Jefferson. **S**	In 1809, James Monroe was the first president inaugurated at the Capitol. **B**	The National Statuary Hall is located in the south wing. **U**	The U.S. Capitol Building is located along the banks of the Mississippi River. **L**
The British set fire to the Capitol during the Civil War. **I**	The U.S. Capitol Building is divided into five levels. **O**	Originally, the Crypt was planned as burial grounds. **T**	Today, the Capitol building contains approximately 47 rooms. **K**
The Statue of Freedom was raised into place in 1863. **R**	The Capitol was originally designed by William Thornton. **N**	The fourth floor includes the chambers of Congress. **E**	The Senate held its first session in its new chamber in 1859. **D**

Unscramble the word using the large bold letters of <u>only</u> the **TRUE** statements.

SENATE

The U.S. Senate is a part of the Legislative Branch of the federal (national) government. The main job of the Legislative Branch is to make laws. Congress is bicameral which means that it is divided into two houses: the Senate and the House of Representatives. Together, these houses are known as Congress.

The structure and role of the U.S. Senate is outlined in the United States Constitution in Article 1. The Senate is referred to as the "upper" house because it has specific powers not granted to the lower house.

Each house has a unique role to make sure that the Legislative Branch fulfills its duties. It is also divided to prevent any one section of the Legislative Branch from becoming unreasonably powerful. The word "senator" comes from the Latin word for "old man."

Congressional Firsts

The first meeting of Congress was in New York City in 1789. Throughout its history, the United States Congress has met in New York City, Philadelphia, and Washington, D.C. The permanent location of Washington D.C. was established by the Residence Act of 1790. The first Senate only had twenty-two members. The first senators elected were Robert Morris and William Maclay from Pennsylvania in 1788. The first former senator to be elected president was James Monroe, America's fifth president. The first female senator was Rebecca Felton, elected in 1992.

Constitutional Requirements

Today, there are one hundred senators at any given time in the Senate. All states have two senators regardless of population or geographic size. There are requirements to be a senator listed in the Constitution. A senator must be 30 years old, must have been a U.S. citizen for at least the last nine years, and must be a legal resident of the state that they are representing.

Senators serve a six-year term. The senator can serve as many terms as they like because there is no term limit, as long as they are re-elected. Every two years, an election for senators is held. In this election, only one-third of the senators will be voted on. This means that the elections are staggered for the Senate.

The head of the Senate is the vice president. However, the vice president's only job in the Senate is to break a tie, should there be a split decision. When the vice president is not breaking a tie, the leader of the

Senate is the president pro tempore. There are also other leadership roles. The majority leader will be elected by senators of the largest political party. The minority leader is elected by the senators who make up the second-largest political party.

Roles and Responsibilities

While the Senate has many different roles and responsibilities, the main task is to vote on new legislation (laws). They do this in conjunction (together) with the House of Representatives. While the House of Representatives has unique powers, so does the Senate. This division of powers helps ensure a system of checks and balances.

The Senate works to operate impeachment hearings. To impeach means to accuse a high-ranking government official of wrong-doing or misconduct while in office. The Senate serves as a court. A two-thirds majority vote is necessary for conviction. If convicted, or declared guilty, the government official may be removed from office. The Senate also has the sole power to ratify (approve) treaties negotiated by the president, which require a two-thirds vote by the Senate.

The Senate also assists the president in picking cabinet members, Supreme Court judges, ambassadors, and military leaders. This is an important check on the power of the Executive Branch. The Senate may hold hearings to question or interview the nominees, perform background checks and reject/approve the nomination.

From Bill to Law

Sometimes, senators want to block or delay a new bill from passing for a variety of reasons. They will prepare a really long speech just to delay it. This strategy of prolonging is called a filibuster. Because there is no limit on how long a debate can be, the senators can take as much time as they need. When it becomes excessively lengthy, three-fifths of the senators can vote to end the speech of that particular senator. This is called cloture. In 1957, Strom Thurmond spoke against the Civil Rights Act, a filibuster attempt that lasted for 24 hours and 18 minutes.

Both houses of Congress must approve the bills in identical form to go into effect. If both houses approve a law, then the president has the opportunity to veto or reject it. Even if there is a veto, the law can be voted on again by Congress. If there is a two-thirds majority vote in both houses, the president's veto is nullified or overridden. This is all part of checks and balances.

MYSTERY MATCH

After reading about the **Senate**, draw a line from the left-hand column to make a match in the right-hand column. Your line should go through **ONE** letter. When you complete all the matches, use the letters with a line THROUGH them to unscramble a mystery word. You MUST start and end your line at the **arrow points**.

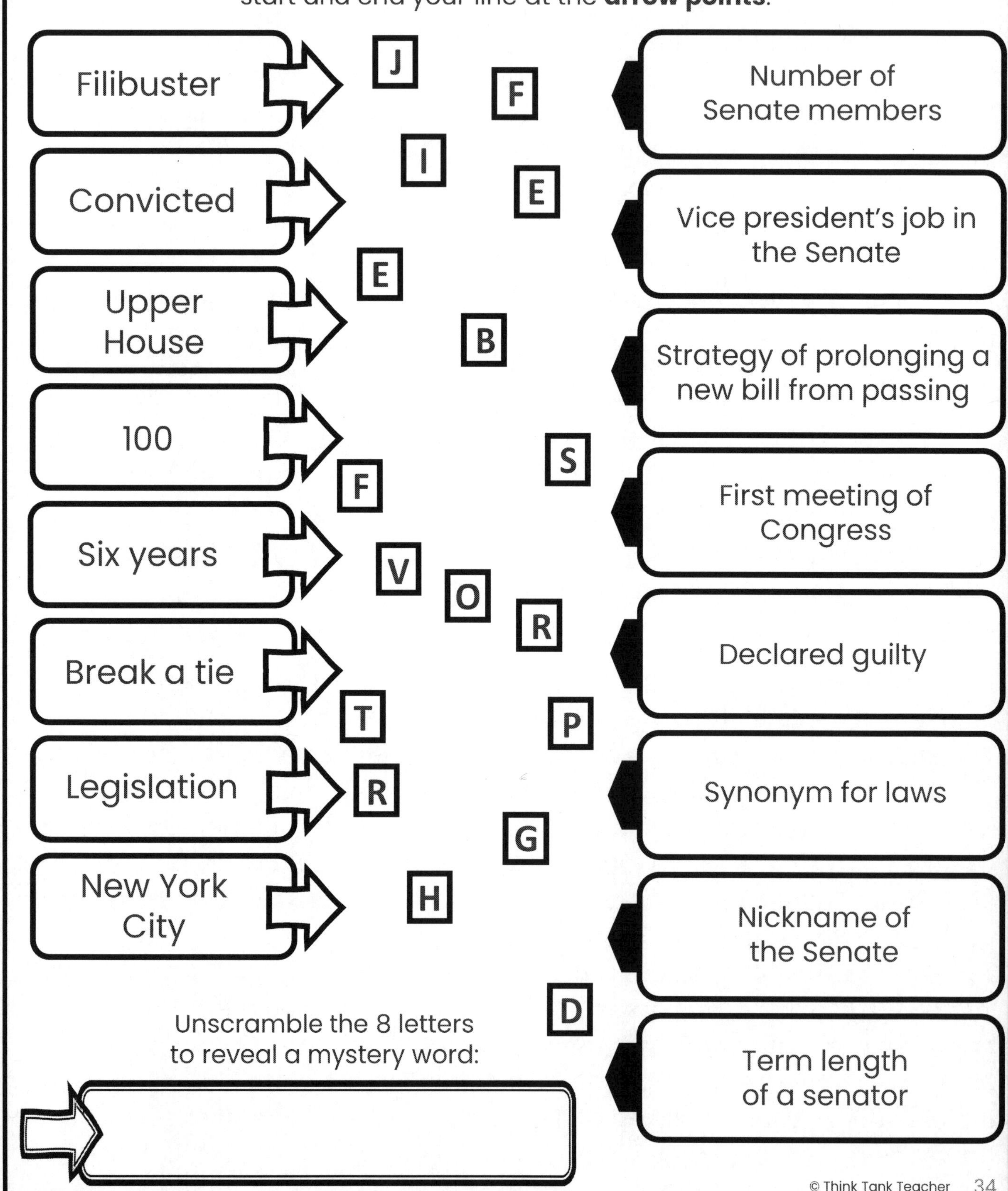

Unscramble the 8 letters to reveal a mystery word:

MULTIPLE CHOICE

After reading about the **Senate**, answer each multiple-choice question below. Then, count the number of times you used each letter as an answer (ABCD) to reveal a 4-digit code. Letters may be used more than once or not at all. If a letter option is not used, put a zero in that box.

1 Regardless of population or geographic size, how many senators does each state have?

A. Two
B. Four
C. Fifty
D. One hundred

2 When the vice president is not breaking a tie, who is the leader of the Senate?

A. Speaker of the House
B. Commander-in-Chief
C. Chief Justice
D. President Pro Tempore

3 Which of the following is a power of the Senate?

A. Approve cabinet members
B. Operate impeachment hearings
C. Ratify treaties
D. All of the above

4 Who was the first former senator to be elected president?

A. George Washington
B. James Monroe
C. James Madison
D. Robert Morris

5 Candidates for the Senate must be U.S. citizens for how long?

A. Last five years
B. Last seven years
C. Last nine years
D. Last twelve years

6 Throughout its history, where has the United States Congress met?

A. Washington D.C.
B. Philadelphia
C. New York City
D. All of the above

7 Which article of the Constitution outlines the role of the Senate?

A. Article I
B. Article II
C. Article III
D. Article IV

8 What is the act when three-fifths of the senators vote to end a long speech?

A. Cloture
B. Filibuster
C. Impeachment
D. Ratification

Count how many times you used each letter as a correct answer (ABCD) to determine the 4-digit code. Record your answer in the boxes below.

# of A's	# of B's	# of C's	# of D's

HOUSE OF REPRESENTATIVES

Article I of the U.S. Constitution is the Legislative Branch, also known as Congress. Congress is bicameral which means that it is made up of two houses: the Senate and the House of Representatives. Each house plays a vital role to ensure that the government is balanced. The main purpose of the House of Representatives is to vote on new legislation (laws) along with various other tasks. The House of Representatives is also known as the "Lower House."

The first meeting of Congress was in New York City in 1789. Throughout its history, the United States Congress has met in New York City, Philadelphia, and Washington, D.C. The permanent location of Washington D.C. was established by the Residence Act of 1790. In the first Congress, the number of House representatives was only sixty-five.

The members of the House of Representatives are elected by the people (constituents) of the state in which they live. Every state has at least one representative, while some states have several. This is based on the population of that state. The states are divided into districts. Each representative can only represent one district. A state with a higher population will have a higher number of representatives. For example, Vermont will have fewer representatives than California.

Changing Populations

If a state's population has changed over the years, it may lose or gain representatives. Regardless of those changes, there can only be four hundred thirty-five members in the House of Representatives at any given time. The representatives are redistributed in each state every ten years to account for the changing populations.

The U.S census, required by the Constitution, is conducted every ten years. The purpose is to provide an accurate count of the population, which in turn informs the House of Representatives when it comes to apportionment (population shifts and representation in each state). The first census in the United States took place in 1790.

Qualifications and Duties

There are qualifications to become a representative listed in the Constitution. The person must be twenty-five years old. They must have lived in the United States for seven years. They also must live in the state that they hope to represent. If they meet these qualifications, the people can elect that person to represent them in the House of Representatives for their district. Once elected, representatives serve a two-year term. There are no term limits in the House, so a person can be a representative repeatedly, as long as they are re-elected.

The representatives have a wide range of tasks once elected. They spend a lot of time working on new bills and making laws. After all, the main purpose of the House is to make new bills and laws. The representatives are responsible for understanding how the new bills or laws could likely impact the area that they represent. The areas of the representatives are all quite different. A law in New York City might have a different impact than in rural Montana. Both the House and the Senate must agree to, vote on, and adopt identical bills in order for a bill to become a law.

The House has extra tasks in addition to making new bills and laws. For example, all tax bills have to start in the House. The House also has the power to impeach high-ranking government officials, like the president or a Supreme Court Justice. To impeach means to accuse or charge with misconduct while in office.

Leadership

The leader of the House is called the Speaker of the House. He or she is next in line to be president after the vice president. The representatives are also required to participate in two committees. Committees focus on a specific issue such as roads or education.

The House of Representatives is able to serve a wide range of areas and diverse (different) groups. If a person has an issue in their district, they can write to or visit their representative's office. Representatives can help their district, specifically in Washington, D.C. They know the needs and wants of the people and businesses. They can apply their local knowledge and advocate (speak up) for the people in Washington. Most representatives have an office in their district as well as in Washington, D.C.

The main responsibilities for the Speaker of the House include presiding (in charge of) over sessions in the House, setting the legislative agenda, and appointing members to committees.

Should no presidential candidate receive a majority of the Electoral College vote, the House of Representatives has the power to choose the next president. This is called a contingent election and is extremely rare.

Nancy Pelosi became the first woman to serve as Speaker of the House in 2007. Joseph Rainey was the first Black American elected to the House in 1870. Jeannette Rankin was the first woman elected to the House in 1916.

TRUE OR FALSE

After reading about the **House of Representatives**, read each statement below and determine if it is true or false. If the statement is true, color the coin that corresponds with that question. If the statement is false, cross out that coin value. When you are finished, add the TOTAL of **ALL TRUE** coin values to reveal a 4-digit code. One digit of the code has been provided for you. If the total is 625, a 6 would go in the first box, the 2 in the second box and so on.

A. Once elected, representatives serve a two-year term.

B. A state with a higher population will have a higher number of representatives.

C. Both the House and the Senate must agree to, vote on, and adopt identical bills in order for a bill to become a law.

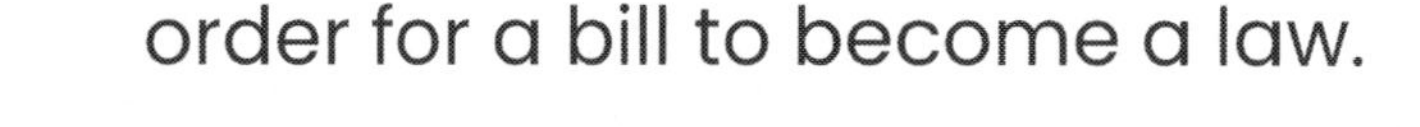

D. The leader of the House is called the Speaker of the House.

E. Jeannette Rankin became the first woman to serve as Speaker of the House in 2007.

F. The representatives are redistributed in each state every ten years to account for the changing populations.

G. To impeach means to accuse or charge with misconduct while in office.

H. Members elected to the House must be thirty-five years old.

After shading the coins based on your answer, add the value of ALL TRUE statements to get the final total. Record your answer in the boxes below.

DOUBLE PUZZLE

After reading about the **House of Representatives**, determine the word that corresponds with the statements provided below. Spell the corresponding word in the boxes to the right. You may or may not use all squares provided for each answer. Any numerical answers must be spelled out. Next, use the numbers **under** indicated letters to reveal a secret word.

1	Last name of the first Black American elected to the House	9 boxes; 6 under box 2
2	The leader of the House is called the ___ of the House	9 boxes; 1 under box 4
3	The representatives are redistributed in each state every ___ years	9 boxes; 7 under box 1
4	The states are divided into ___	9 boxes; 2 under box 1
5	The House of Representatives is also known as the "___ House"	9 boxes
6	An accurate count of the population required by the Constitution	9 boxes; 5 under box 1
7	Number of years for the term length of a representative	9 boxes
8	Representatives must have lived in the U.S. for ___ years	9 boxes; 3 under box 3
9	Last name of the first woman to serve as Speaker of the House	9 boxes; 8 under box 2
10	Synonym for constituents in the state in which they live	9 boxes; 4 under box 3

SECRET WORD

1	2	3	4	5	6	7	8

FROM BILL TO LAW

Roughly twenty-five thousand bills are presented to Congress each term, but less than ten percent of those bills become law. The first bill introduced in Congress was on May 19, 1789. The bill dealt with setting up the process for administering the oaths of office to government officials.

Introducing the Bill

A bill can start in either the House or Senate. However, bills about money must begin in the House of Representatives. The process of making a bill a law starts with an idea. Congress, the president, and even outside groups or people (constituents) can draft (write) a bill. Only a member of Congress, however, can formally introduce and sponsor a bill.

Once a bill has been drafted, the sponsor introduces the bill to the floor of the House or Senate. At this point, the bill is printed in the Congressional Record and is assigned a number. The sponsor places the bill in a wooden box next to the clerk's desk called the "hopper."

The Committee Process

Regardless of where the bill originated, that chamber sends the bill to a committee (a group of experts in a specific area). The committee then determines the pros and cons of the bill. Various committees analyze bills, based on the subject matter. For instance, the education committee would examine a bill about schools. The committee will study the bill, often by holding hearings where experts, government officials, or members of the public can provide input.

Committees can amend the bill by suggesting changes to the bill. Once the bill has been analyzed, committee members vote on the bill. If the committee approves the bill, it moves to the full House or Senate for debate. If the bill is not approved by the committee, it often "dies" there and goes no further. Ninety percent of bills "die" in committee.

If the bill passes, it moves to the Rules Committee. The Rules Committee determines the date for the debate and the rules for debating the bill. The length and rules for debate vary between the House and Senate.

Debate and Voting

If a majority of members in the House or Senate vote in favor of the bill, it moves to the other chamber for consideration. If the bill passes in the House, a senator introduces the bill in the Senate. The same process of committee review, debate, and voting takes place. If the majority votes in favor of the bill, the bill moves to the entire Senate for debate.

The House or Senate can reject any changes to the bill. If a chamber rejects any changes, a conference committee (with members from the House and Senate) works on a compromise. The House and Senate then vote on the changes made by the conference committee. Once a compromise is reached, the revised bill is sent back to both chambers for approval. Both the House and the Senate must pass the exact same version of the bill.

Filibusters and Cloture

The Senate can stall the bill at this point by delivering a lengthy speech called a filibuster. Today, the filibuster is not often used. Strom Thurmond, a senator from South Carolina, filibustered the Civil Rights Act of 1957 for just over twenty-four hours. This is the longest single-person filibuster in Senate history. Another famous filibuster happened when senators talked for a record 72 days before the Civil Rights Act of 1964 was finally passed.

A cloture motion of the Senate would be needed to stop the filibuster. If enough senators (three-fifths) agree to cloture, it means the talking must end, and the Senate can move forward with voting on the bill.

The President's Role

The president takes action with an approval or rejection of the bill. The president has ten days to sign a bill into law. If he/she approves, they will sign the bill into law. If he/she rejects it, they will not sign the bill, effectively vetoing (denying) it. With a veto, the bill can still become law. The vetoed bill is sent back to Congress where both the House and Senate vote once again. If two-thirds of both houses vote to override the veto, it becomes a law. If the president does nothing for ten days while Congress is in session, the bill automatically becomes law, without a signature. If Congress adjourns during this ten-day period and the president takes no action, the bill dies. This is called a pocket veto.

The first bill vetoed by a U.S. President was in 1792. President George Washington vetoed a bill regarding the apportionment (distribution) of seats in the House of Representatives. Another important veto happened in 1866. The Civil Rights Act of 1866, which was created to protect the rights of Black Americans after the Civil War, was vetoed by President Andrew Johnson. However, Congress overrode the veto and the bill became law, paving the way for the 14th Amendment, which ensures equal protection under the law. Johnson was America's seventeenth president.

PARAGRAPH CODE

After reading about **Bill to Law**, head back to the reading and number ALL the paragraphs in the reading passage. Then, read each statement below and determine which paragraph **NUMBER** the statement can be found in. Paragraph numbers MAY be used more than one time or not at all. Follow the directions below to reveal the 4-digit code.

A Both the House and the Senate must pass the exact same version of the bill.

B If the bill is not approved by the committee, it often "dies" there and goes no further.

C The sponsor places the bill in a wooden box next to the clerk's desk called the "hopper."

D Once a bill has been drafted, the sponsor introduces the bill to the floor of the House or Senate.

E Washington vetoed a bill regarding the apportionment (distribution) of seats in the House of Representatives.

F If enough senators (three-fifths) agree to cloture, it means the talking must end, and the Senate can move forward with voting on the bill.

G Congress, the president, and even outside groups or people (constituents) can draft (write) a bill.

H The Senate can stall the bill at this point by delivering a lengthy speech called a filibuster.

ELIMINATE ALL EVEN-NUMBERED paragraphs that you used as an answer. Record the remaining numbers (in the SAME order in which you recorded them above) in the boxes below.

MYSTERY WORD

After reading about **Bill to Law**, determine if each statement below is true or false. Color or shade the boxes of the **TRUE** statements. Next, unscramble the mystery word using the large letters of the **TRUE** statements.

Only fourteen percent of bills "die" in committee. **H**	Cloture requires a one-third vote in the House. **P**	Bills about money must begin in the House of Representatives. **T**	A cloture motion of the Senate would be needed to stop the filibuster. **M**
If two-thirds of both houses vote to override the veto, it becomes a law. **T**	The Civil Rights Act of 1866 was vetoed by President Abraham Lincoln. **D**	Johnson was America's seventeenth president. **M**	Committees can amend the bill by suggesting changes to the bill. **E**
The Rules Committee determines the date for the debate. **I**	The president has twenty days to sign a bill into law. **N**	The first bill vetoed by a U.S. President was in 1792. **O**	Conference committees include members from both houses. **E**
Today, the filibuster is frequently used. **A**	Strom Thurmond filibustered the Civil Rights Act of 1957 for six days. **S**	Any person can formally introduce and sponsor a bill. **B**	The first bill introduced in Congress was on May 19, 1789. **C**

Unscramble the word using the large bold letters of only the **TRUE** statements.

POWERS OF CONGRESS

The United States Congress, or Legislative Branch, includes the Senate and the House of Representatives. Legislation (making laws) is one of the chief powers of Congress, but it has many other non-legislative (non-lawmaking) duties as well.

The two houses of Congress represent the people of the United States. The Senate is made up of two representatives per state elected to stand for the important issues. The Senate has had one hundred members since the most recent state, Hawaii, became a state in 1959. The vice president is the leader of the Senate and is the tie-breaking vote if ever there is a 50-50 split on a decision.

The House of Representatives is based upon the population of each state. There have been four hundred thirty-five representatives in the House of Representatives since 1910. There are several states with only one representative such as Alaska, Delaware, and Wyoming. The states with the most representatives are California, Texas, and Florida. The Speaker of the House (leader) is elected by the other members of the House. This person becomes third in the line of succession to become president should something happen to both the current president and vice president.

The powers of Congress are listed in the Constitution, and they can be divided into three main types: legislative powers, financial powers, and oversight powers. Article I outlines over twenty powers of Congress.

Legislative Powers

The main power of Congress is to create and pass laws. Before a law is passed, it starts as an idea that becomes a bill. Both the House and the Senate must agree on the bill before it goes to the president to be signed into law. At this point, the president has the authority to veto (reject) the bill if he/she does not think it should be law. If he/she does that, the bill goes back to Congress. If it reaches a two-thirds majority vote in both houses, it becomes law without the president's signature.

Only Congress can declare war on another country, although many people mistakenly believe the president holds this power. Even though the president is the commander-in-chief of the military, Congress has the final say on declaring war.

Congress has the power to regulate and control trade, both within the United States and between the U.S. and other countries. This is called interstate and foreign commerce.

Congress is also responsible for immigration and naturalization laws, meaning that Congress decides the rules for who can come to the United States and how people can become U.S. citizens.

Specific Chamber Powers

Each chamber has unique powers. For instance, the president can appoint (choose) people to lead government departments or serve as judges, but the Senate must approve these choices before they can take office. The Senate is responsible for ratifying (approving) treaties with foreign governments. The Senate may also choose the vice president if there is no majority in the Electoral College.

Powers of the House of Representatives include tax and spending bills and the impeachment of high-ranking government officials. To impeach means to accuse of misconduct in office. The House is also responsible for choosing the president if there is no majority in the Electoral College.

Financial Powers

Congress has control over all government spending. This is one of the most important ways Congress can make sure the government is working properly and responsibly. Congress has the authority to set and collect taxes. These taxes pay for things like roads, schools, and national defense. If the government needs more money than it has, Congress can allow the U.S. to borrow money, which adds to the national debt. Congress also works with the president to create a budget, which is a plan for how the government will spend its money each year.

Oversight Powers

Congress is responsible for making sure the government is following the law and that federal agencies are doing their jobs properly. This is called oversight. Congress uses several tools to keep an eye on the government. Congress can remove government officials, like the president, from office if they break the law or misuse their power.

Congress has additional powers that do not fit neatly into the other categories, but they are still important. Congress has the power to establish and regulate post offices. While the president commands the military, Congress controls the funding and makes decisions about the size and structure of the armed forces. Congress also has the power to admit new states into the Union and control U.S. territories. Congress can create lower federal courts and make all laws necessary and proper to carry out the expressed (written) or enumerated powers.

MYSTERY MATCH

After reading about the **Powers of Congress**, draw a line from the left-hand column to make a match in the right-hand column. Your line should go through **ONE** letter. When you complete all the matches, use the letters with a line THROUGH them to unscramble a mystery word. You MUST start and end your line at the **arrow points**.

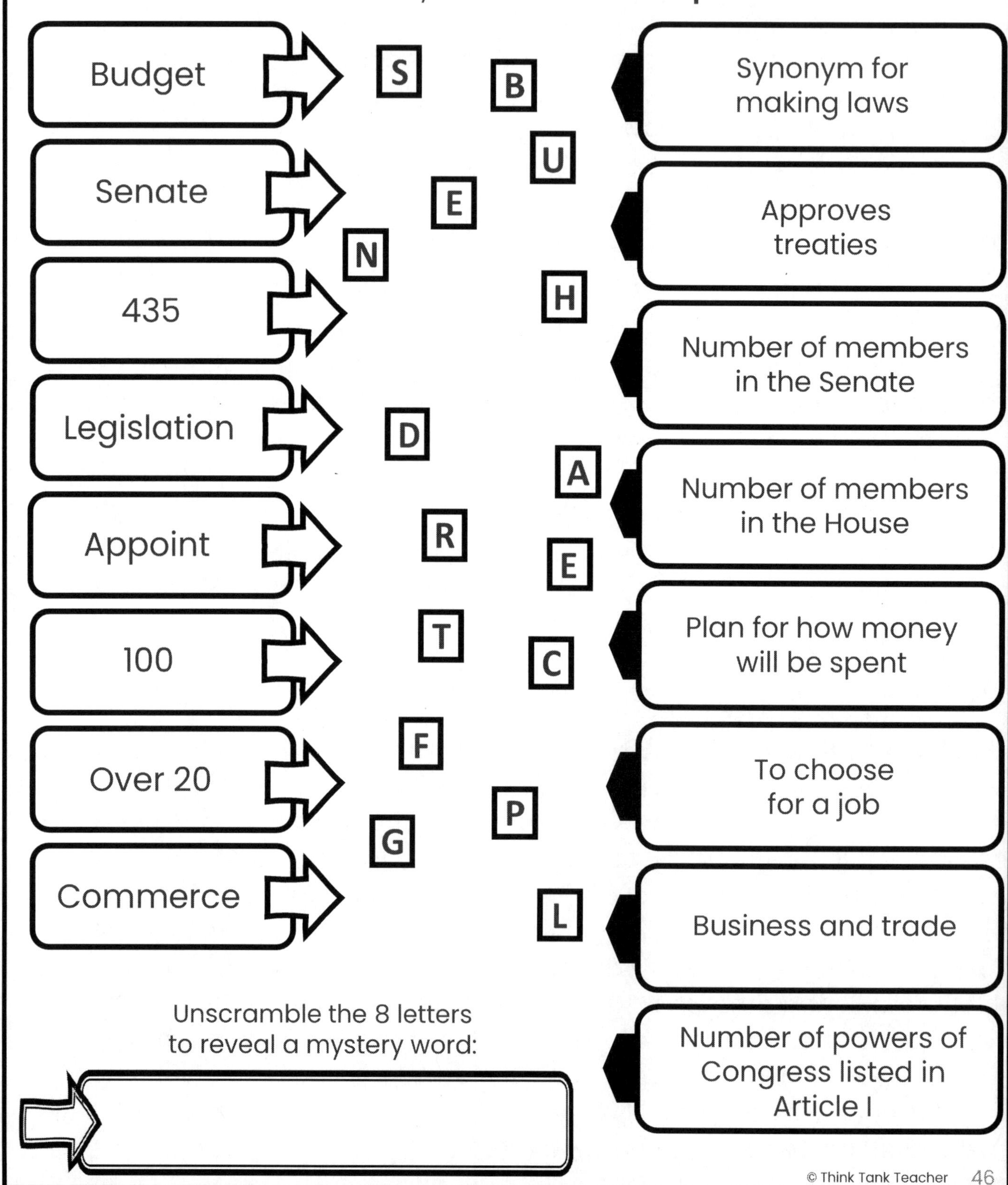

Unscramble the 8 letters to reveal a mystery word:

MULTIPLE CHOICE

After reading about the **Powers of Congress**, answer each multiple-choice question below. Then, count the number of times you used each letter as an answer (ABCD) to reveal a 4-digit code. Letters may be used more than once or not at all. If a letter option is not used, put a zero in that box.

1 How many representatives in the House does each state have?

A. Two
B. Six
C. Twenty
D. Depends on the population

2 Where do all tax and spending bills begin?

A. Senate
B. House of Representatives
C. Supreme Court
D. Rules Committee

3 What leader of the Senate is responsible for breaking a tie?

A. Speaker of the House
B. Vice president
C. Secretary of State
D. Commander-in-chief

4 Who will choose the vice president if there is no majority in the Electoral College?

A. President
B. Senate
C. Supreme Court
D. House of Representatives

5 Which of the following is NOT a power of Congress?

A. Establish post offices
B. Admit new states to the Union
C. Veto laws
D. Create lower federal courts

6 What branch of government is the U.S. Congress a part of?

A. Legislative Branch
B. Executive Branch
C. Judicial Branch
D. Parliament Branch

7 What are federal taxes used to pay for?

A. National defense
B. Roads
C. Schools
D. All of the above

8 Which of the following is NOT a power of Congress?

A. Regulate and control trade
B. Determine if laws are constitutional
C. Create immigration laws
D. Declare war

Count how many times you used each letter as a correct answer (ABCD) to determine the 4-digit code. Record your answer in the boxes below.

# of A's	# of B's	# of C's	# of D's

ARTICLE II

EXECUTIVE BRANCH

Each branch of the federal (national) government has unique responsibilities. The federal government is structured and designed this way to prevent any one branch of the government from becoming too powerful.

The Executive Branch refers to the offices of the president and vice-president and has many different purposes. However, its main purpose is to carry out and enforce laws. This branch, also known as Article II, makes sure that the laws of the United States are being followed and obeyed.

The president of the United States is the leader of the Executive Branch. There are several people that operate underneath the president to help him. These people include the vice president and the cabinet. The president's cabinet is a critical piece of the Executive Branch because it offers advice and information to the president. The cabinet is a group of advisors that specialize in certain areas like education or defense. The cabinet includes fifteen different departments such as the Department of Education, Department of Agriculture, Department of Energy, and the Department of Defense. George Washington's cabinet only had four members, so it has grown over time.

Responsibilities of the President

The president is the leader of the United States, also known as Head of State. It is his or her job to make sure the country is operating smoothly and fairly. The president has many responsibilities, one is to approve or veto (reject) new laws from Congress (Legislative Branch). The president also enforces laws that have already been passed. The president can appoint (choose) Supreme Court judges and cabinet members with consent (approval) by the Senate.

The president is also the Commander-in-Chief of the military. Many mistakenly believe that the president can declare war but only Congress has that power. The president is the chief diplomat, which means he works with other countries to negotiate peace treaties and trade agreements.

Presidential Terms and Qualifications

The position of the president is limited to a maximum of two four-year terms. In 1951, the 22nd Amendment was added to the Constitution, preventing any one president from serving more than two consecutive terms. Consecutive means one after another. This was to make sure that this branch of government could not become too powerful in the hands of one person. This amendment was added after Franklin D. Roosevelt was elected to four terms as president, during the Great Depression and after the outbreak of World War II in 1939.

The U.S. Constitution includes three requirements to become president. Candidates must be thirty-five years old, must have been born in the United States, as well as lived in the U.S. for at least fourteen years. The vice-president must also meet the requirements to be president.

The line of succession indicates who will take over should something happen to the standing president. It starts with the vice president, who is first in line to the presidency. If the vice president is unable to take on the role, the Speaker of the House of Representatives is next in line. After that is the Senate leader, followed by a specific order of cabinet members.

Under the president, is the vice president. The vice president is ready to help the president with any task at any time. The vice president is responsible for breaking a tie in the Senate because there is an even number of senators (one hundred). When the VP is not breaking a tie, the president pro tempore serves as head of the Senate.

The president lives in the White House and the vice-president lives in a mansion at the U.S. Naval Observatory. Both work in Washington, D.C. in the West Wing of the White House.

State of the Union Address and the EOP

Each year, the State of the Union Address typically takes place in late January or early February. Article II, Section 3 of the Constitution requires the president "from time to time give to the Congress information of the State of the Union."

The president has a team called the Executive Office of the President, or the "EOP." This office was created by Franklin D. Roosevelt in 1939 to help the president fulfill the endless tasks. The EOP is responsible for advising the president on national security issues and intelligence issues. Another role of the EOP is the White House Communications and Press Secretary. The Press Secretary gives briefings to the media to keep Americans informed about what the president is doing.

The president makes various speeches and appearances during his term, sometimes addressing the economic situation of the U.S. He or she also give interviews and visit areas of the nation that are facing some type of major hardship, such as a hurricane. The president is known worldwide because of how he negotiates and represents the U.S. with other countries.

TRUE OR FALSE

After reading about the **Executive Branch**, read each statement below and determine if it is true or false. If the statement is true, color the coin that corresponds with that question. If the statement is false, cross out that coin value. When you are finished, add the TOTAL of **ALL TRUE** coin values to reveal a 4-digit code. One digit of the code has been provided for you. If the total is 625, a 6 would go in the first box, the 2 in the second box and so on.

A. The vice president is responsible for breaking a tie in the Senate.

B. The president can appoint Supreme Court judges and cabinet members with consent by the Senate.

B 25

C. George Washington's cabinet had forty members, so it has shrunk over time.

F 75

D. The U.S. Constitution includes five requirements to become president.

E. If the vice president is unable to take on the role of president, the Secretary of Defense is next in line.

F. The 24th Amendment prevented any one president from serving more than two consecutive terms.

G. The position of the president is limited to a maximum of four six-year terms.

H. The cabinet is a group of advisors that specialize in certain areas like education or defense.

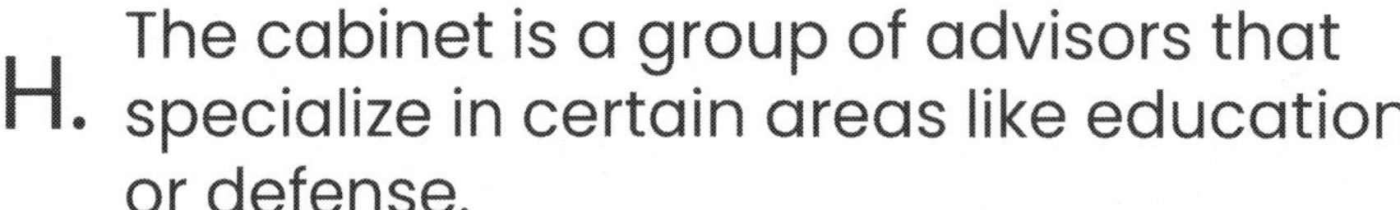

After shading the coins based on your answer, add the value of ALL TRUE statements to get the final total. Record your answer in the boxes below.

DOUBLE PUZZLE

After reading about the **Executive Branch**, determine the word that corresponds with the statements provided below. Spell the corresponding word in the boxes to the right. You may or may not use all squares provided for each answer. Any numerical answers must be spelled out. Next, use the numbers **under** indicated letters to reveal a secret word.

1	Number of requirements listed in the Constitution for presidential candidates	9 boxes; 5 under box 3
2	The ___ Secretary gives briefings to the media	9 boxes; 7 under box 3
3	Synonym for federal	9 boxes; 2 under box 1
4	Presidential appointments of judges must be approved by the ___	9 boxes; 8 under box 1
5	EOP stands for the Executive ___ of the President	9 boxes
6	Number of years for one presidential term	9 boxes; 3 under box 1
7	When the VP is not breaking a tie, the head of the Senate is the president pro ___	9 boxes
8	Group of advisors to the president	9 boxes; 6 under box 1
9	The president works in the ___ Wing of the White House	9 boxes; 1 under box 2
10	Number of years presidential candidates must live in the U.S.	9 boxes; 4 under box 2

SECRET WORD

1	2	3	4	5	6	7	8

WHITE HOUSE

The White House is one of the most iconic buildings in the world, serving as the home and workplace of every U.S. president since John Adams in 1800. Located at 1600 Pennsylvania Avenue in Washington, D.C., it stands as a symbol of the American presidency and the Executive Branch of the U.S. government.

History of the White House

Construction of the White House began in 1792, after President George Washington selected the site. Washington oversaw the construction but never lived in the White House. It was designed by an architect named James Hoban and completed in 1800. John Adams (America's second president) became the first president to reside in it. The mansion was designed in a neoclassical style, with influences from both Georgian and Roman architecture.

Originally, the building was called the "President's Palace" or "Executive Mansion." It was not officially named the White House until 1901, when President Theodore Roosevelt gave it the name we use today.

The War of 1812 and the Burning of the White House

One of the most dramatic moments in the White House's history occurred during the War of 1812. In 1814, British troops invaded Washington, D.C., and set fire to multiple government buildings, including the White House. First Lady Dolley Madison, wife of President James Madison, famously saved a portrait of George Washington before fleeing. The mansion was severely damaged, and only the exterior walls remained.

After the war, James Hoban was hired once again to rebuild the White House, and it was restored by 1817, just in time for President James Monroe to move in.

Presidential Firsts in the White House

Over the years, the White House has been the site of many "firsts" for U.S. presidents. James Monroe was the first president to hold an inaugural ball at the White House in 1829. Abraham Lincoln signed the Emancipation Proclamation here in 1863. William Howard Taft installed the first Oval Office in 1909. Franklin D. Roosevelt was the first president to broadcast a speech (his famous "fireside chats") from the White House over the radio in the 1930s. In 2009, Barack Obama became the first Black American president to live in the White House. In 1891, President Benjamin Harrison had electricity added to the house for the first time. During Jimmy Carter's term (1977-1981), the first computer was installed in the White House.

The White House Today

The White House is much larger than it looks from the outside. It has one hundred thirty-two rooms, including thirty-five bathrooms, twenty-eight fireplaces, eight staircases, and three elevators. In addition to the family living quarters, the building houses offices, meeting rooms, and spaces for official ceremonies and events. The building has a swimming pool, bowling alley, and a movie theater.

One of the most famous rooms in the White House is the Oval Office, where the president works and meets with world leaders. This room has been the setting for historic decisions and speeches. The Oval Office is located in the West Wing, which was built in 1902 during Theodore Roosevelt's presidency. Every president since has added their own personal touches to the room, including the desk they use, known as the Resolute Desk. In 1824 and 1829, President John Quincy Adams added the South and North Porticoes (the fancy entrances) to the White House.

The East and West Wings

The White House is divided into three main sections: the Executive Residence, the East Wing, and the West Wing. The Executive Residence is where the president and their family live. It also contains the State Dining Room, Blue Room, and Red Room, which are used for official events. The West Wing contains the president's offices, including the Oval Office, the Cabinet Room, and the Situation Room, which is used for crisis management and military operations. The East Wing contains the offices of the First Lady and is often used for hosting tours and events.

The White House Grounds

The White House sits on eighteen acres of beautifully landscaped grounds, including the South Lawn and the Rose Garden. The South Lawn is where the president often arrives by helicopter (Marine One) and is used for various public events. The Rose Garden, located just outside the Oval Office, is often used for press conferences and official announcements.

Over the years, the White House has not only been the home of the president but also a major historic landmark. It welcomes millions of visitors each year, whether they are tourists touring the public rooms or heads of state attending official functions.

PARAGRAPH CODE

After reading about the **White House**, head back to the reading and number ALL the paragraphs in the reading passage. Then, read each statement below and determine which paragraph **NUMBER** the statement can be found in. Paragraph numbers MAY be used more than one time or not at all. Follow the directions below to reveal the 4-digit code.

A First Lady Dolley Madison, wife of President James Madison, famously saved a portrait of George Washington before fleeing.

B The White House sits on eighteen acres of beautifully landscaped grounds, including the South Lawn and the Rose Garden.

C It also contains the State Dining Room, Blue Room, and Red Room, which are used for official events.

D The building has a swimming pool, bowling alley, and a movie theater.

E Construction of the White House began in 1792, after President George Washington selected the site.

F The East Wing contains the offices of the First Lady and is often used for hosting tours and events.

G In 1891, President Benjamin Harrison had electricity added to the house for the first time.

H Originally, the building was called the "President's Palace" or "Executive Mansion."

ELIMINATE ALL EVEN-NUMBERED paragraphs that you used as an answer. Record the remaining numbers (in the SAME order in which you recorded them above) in the boxes below.

MYSTERY WORD

After reading about the **White House**, determine if each statement below is true or false. Color or shade the boxes of the **TRUE** statements. Next, unscramble the mystery word using the large letters of the **TRUE** statements.

The president's helicopter is known as Air Force One. **A**	The White House was designed by an architect named Frédéric Auguste Bartholdi. **T**	The Situation Room is used for crisis management and military operations. **D**	The White House has two hundred twenty-two rooms. **F**
The White House has three elevators. **I**	Ronald Reagan had electricity added to the house for the first time. **O**	Jimmy Carter served as president from 1997-2001. **H**	President John Quincy Adams added the South and North Porticoes. **E**
In 1814, British troops set fire to multiple government buildings. **E**	The East Wing contains the offices of the First Lady. **R**	Washington oversaw the construction but never lived in the White House. **C**	The White House is located at 1600 Pennsylvania Avenue. **N**
The Oval Office is located in the West Wing. **E**	The South Lawn is where the president often arrives by helicopter. **S**	The Oval Office was built in 1902 during McKinley's presidency. **P**	The White House sits on forty acres of landscaped grounds. **L**

Unscramble the word using the large bold letters of <u>only</u> the **TRUE** statements.

PRESIDENT'S CABINET

The president is the head of the Executive Branch of the federal (national) government. The Executive Branch is outlined in Article II of the U.S. Constitution. The word "cabinet" cannot be found in the U.S. Constitution; but it does say that the president can appoint (choose) "principal officers" of "executive departments." The term "cabinet" originated from a French or Italian word meaning "small, private room." James Madison first described the meetings of his advisors as the "president's cabinet."

A "cabinet" of people helps the president make informed decisions about a wide range of topics. The people who make up the president's cabinet each have a special set of skills and serve as advisors. The members of the cabinet operate out of the White House in Washington, D.C.

The cabinet is organized by the president. The members are not elected by citizens. The president appoints, or chooses, his or her cabinet members, then they are confirmed (approved) by the Senate. The president can instate (set up) and remove members as he/she sees fit. The head of the cabinet is the vice president.

History of the Cabinet

The cabinet is typically made up of fifteen departments. When the president meets with the cabinet, they sit in a very traditional way, based on when their department was formed. The department heads (leaders) of the oldest departments sit closest to the president, while the newest department heads sit further away. The oldest cabinet positions are the Department of State and the Department of Treasury. Cabinet heads include the title of secretary, such as the Secretary of Education, except for the Department of Justice which has the title of Attorney General. The Judiciary Act of 1789 created the office of Attorney General.

George Washington was the first president to organize and use a cabinet. His cabinet included four advisors and first met on November 26, 1791. Members included Secretary of State Thomas Jefferson, Secretary of the Treasury Alexander Hamilton, Secretary of War Henry Knox, and Attorney General Edmund Randolph. The cabinet has remained very similar in operation and function to this day.

Role of the Cabinet

Some presidents have created subcommittees under the cabinet members to discuss complex issues. This helps the president make the most informed decisions. The cabinet members are heads of a wide range of departments. This allows other parts of the government to continue to function under the leadership of the cabinet members, while the president sees to more challenging issues. For example, if there is a major problem with the banking system, the Secretary of the Treasury would help the president work to solve the problem. The president would be able to focus specifically on this issue, while the other cabinet members see to the operation of the rest of the government.

Vice President John Adams did not attend Washington's cabinet meetings because he was considered a "legislative officer." It was not until the 20th Century that vice-presidents could attended cabinet meetings.

Cabinet Departments

The Department of Agriculture oversees food and farming. The Department of Commerce works on promoting the economy. The Department of Defense oversees the military and is the largest department. The Department of Education handles schools and education. The Department of Energy oversees energy research. The Department of Health and Human Services focuses on keeping Americans healthy.

The Department of Homeland Security (formed in 2002) works to prevent terrorism. The Department of Housing and Urban Development focuses on housing needs. The Department of the Interior oversees national parks, wildlife, natural resources, and land. The Department of Justice enforces laws and protects the public. The Department of Labor focuses on jobs and employment. The Department of State handles international relationships with other countries. The Department of Transportation oversees transportation. The Department of the Treasury oversees the financial system. The Department of Veteran's Affairs oversees benefit programs created for the country's veterans.

Cabinet Firsts

Frances Perkins was the first female cabinet member appointed by President Franklin D. Roosevelt in 1933. Perkins served as the Secretary of Labor. In 1966, President Lyndon B. Johnson appointed Robert C. Weaver as the first Black American to serve in the cabinet. Colin Powell was the first Black American to serve as Secretary of State. Lauro Cavazos became the first Hispanic cabinet member in 1988 as the Secretary of Education. Norman Mineta became the first Asian American cabinet member as the Secretary of Commerce.

MYSTERY MATCH

After reading about the **President's Cabinet**, draw a line from the left-hand column to make a match in the right-hand column. Your line should go through **ONE** letter. When you complete all the matches, use the letters with a line THROUGH them to unscramble a mystery word. You MUST start and end your line at the **arrow points**.

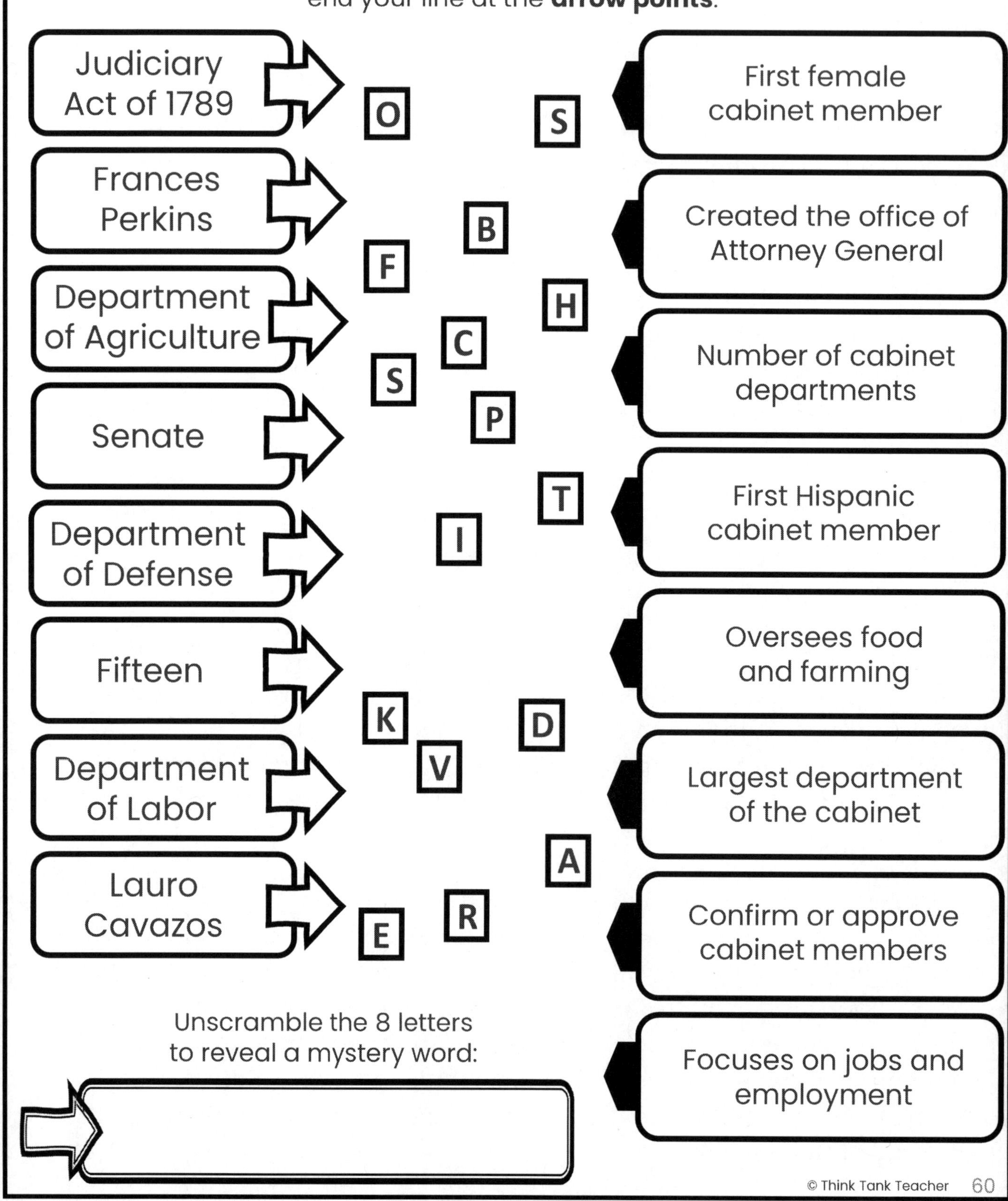

Unscramble the 8 letters to reveal a mystery word:

MULTIPLE CHOICE

After reading about the **President's Cabinet**, answer each multiple-choice question below. Then, count the number of times you used each letter as an answer (ABCD) to reveal a 4-digit code. Letters may be used more than once or not at all. If a letter option is not used, put a zero in that box.

1 What department handles international relationships with other countries?

A. Department of State
B. Department of Exterior
C. Department of Interior
D. Department of Commerce

2 Norman Mineta became the first Asian American cabinet member to serve in what role?

A. Secretary of Education
B. Secretary of Commerce
C. Attorney General
D. Secretary of State

3 Which department works on promoting the economy?

A. Commerce
B. Treasury
C. Labor
D. Interior

4 Who was the first Black American to serve as Secretary of State?

A. Colin Powell
B. Frances Perkins
C. Robert Weaver
D. Norman Mineta

5 Who was Washington's Secretary of War?

A. Henry Knox
B. Alexander Hamilton
C. Thomas Jefferson
D. Frances Perkins

6 Which department works to prevent terrorism?

A. Housing and Urban Development
B. Homeland Security
C. Commerce
D. Labor

7 Who first described the meetings of his advisors as the "president's cabinet"?

A. George Washington
B. Thomas Jefferson
C. John Adams
D. James Madison

8 Which department head has the title of Attorney General?

A. Justice
B. Labor
C. Education
D. Homeland Security

Count how many times you used each letter as a correct answer (ABCD) to determine the 4-digit code. Record your answer in the boxes below.

# of A's

# of B's

# of C's

# of D's

PRESIDENTIAL ELECTIONS

In the United States, every four years we elect the next President of the United States (POTUS). There are rules about who can be elected president, how long they can remain president, and regulations about their job duties during their time in office.

Requirements to Become President

The U.S. Constitution outlines three requirements to become president. The first requirement says a potential candidate must be a natural-born citizen (born in the United States). The second requirement states that candidates have to live in the U.S. for at least fourteen years. Lastly, the president can be no younger than thirty-five years old when he or she takes office. The founders of the United States thought this would ensure someone who is mature and able to effectively run the country would be the POTUS. The 22nd Amendment of the Constitution outlines presidential term limits, which is two terms, or eight years.

The POTUS is the head of the Executive Branch and Commander-in-Chief of the armed forces (military). The Executive Branch is responsible for carrying out and enforcing the laws. This branch works together with two other branches of government; the Legislative Branch (makes laws) and the Judicial Branch (interprets laws).

The president is responsible for appointing officials such as cabinet leaders. The cabinet is a group of presidential advisors. The president also has the power to veto legislation (laws) passed by Congress, although Congress can override a veto with a two-thirds vote. Additionally, the president has the power to negotiate treaties with foreign governments, subject to the consent (approval) of the Senate. Another significant power is the ability to issue executive orders. These orders are directives issued by the president that have the force of law, but do not require approval from Congress.

The Election Process

When a candidate fits the terms for being president outlined in the Constitution, they must run for office in an election. U.S. citizens hold the power of voting for the next president. Candidates do their best to tell the citizens why they should vote for them and how they would run the country if they were elected POTUS. Everyone who is a citizen of the United States, over the age of eighteen and has registered to vote, can vote in a presidential election. Each state has its own requirements for voter registration. In some states, voters are automatically registered when they get a driver's license or state ID.

Primaries and Political Parties

Once a candidate decides to run in a presidential election, there are primaries to narrow down the competition. Each political party, Democrats, Republicans, Independents, the Green Party, and others all have their own candidates they believe would be the best fit for the job of POTUS.

There are two types of primary elections: open and closed. A closed primary means that only members that belong to that particular political party can cast a vote. An open primary means that voters that do not belong to a party can vote. In the end, the political parties will only nominate one candidate for president to represent their party on the general election ballot. In some cases, states hold caucuses rather than primaries, which involve a more complex process of selecting delegates.

The Republican and Democratic parties hold national conventions to formally nominate their candidate for president. Delegates from each state vote to determine the party's nominee. The candidate with the most delegates is typically chosen, though there are some exceptions.

At national conventions, the presidential candidate chooses a running-mate or vice president. The chosen candidates then begin the campaign process traveling across the country. This allows candidates to explain their views and try to win the support of voters. Each political party has a committee which raises money for the campaign and TV commercials.

Election Day

The general election for POTUS happens in November every four years. Election Day is held the first Tuesday after the first Monday in November. Congress officially declared Election Day in 1845.

The Electoral College

In the U.S., the vote for president is not based on the popular vote, or who earns the most votes. Instead, it is based on the Electoral College and its votes. There are 538 electors in the Electoral College. Each state has a minimum of three electors. Each elector casts one electoral vote following the general election. A majority of 270 electoral votes is needed to win the presidency. It is possible to win the popular vote, but not win the presidency based on how the Electoral College votes. The newly elected president and vice president take the oath of office and are inaugurated in January.

TRUE OR FALSE

After reading about **Presidential Elections**, read each statement below and determine if it is true or false. If the statement is true, color the coin that corresponds with that question. If the statement is false, cross out that coin value. When you are finished, add the TOTAL of **ALL TRUE** coin values to reveal a 4-digit code. One digit of the code has been provided for you. If the total is 625, a 6 would go in the first box, the 2 in the second box and so on.

A. The 18th Amendment of the Constitution outlines presidential term limits.

B. A closed primary means that voters that do not belong to a party can vote.

C. Each political party has a committee which raises money for the campaign and TV commercials.

D. In some states, voters are automatically registered when they get a driver's license or state ID.

E. Election Day is held the first Tuesday after the first Monday in November.

F. There are 538 electors in the Electoral College.

G. Presidential candidates have to live in the U.S. for at least twenty years.

H. At national conventions, the presidential candidate chooses a running-mate or vice president.

After shading the coins based on your answer, add the value of ALL TRUE statements to get the final total. Record your answer in the boxes below.

9

DOUBLE PUZZLE

After reading about **Presidential Elections**, determine the word that corresponds with the statements provided below. Spell the corresponding word in the boxes to the right. You may or may not use all squares provided for each answer. Any numerical answers must be spelled out. Next, use the numbers **under** indicated letters to reveal a secret word.

#	Statement	1	2	3	4	5	6	7	8	9
1	The month Election Day occurs	8				3				
2	Minimum number of electors in each state									
3	Minimum age to vote		6							
4	Number of terms a president can serve									
5	There are two types of ___ elections: open and closed	4								
6	Group of presidential advisors		2							
7	Synonym for armed forces						5			
8	Some states hold ___ rather than primaries				1					
9	Number of presidential requirements outlined in the Constitution									
10	___ officially declared Election Day in 1845				7					

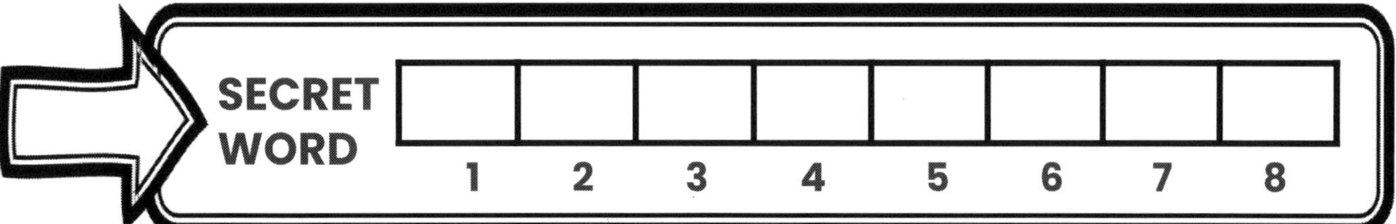

STATE OF THE UNION ADDRESS

Each year, the State of the Union Address typically takes place in late January or early February. Article II, Section 3 of the United States Constitution requires the president "from time to time give to the Congress information of the State of the Union."

The Founding Fathers included this requirement to ensure that the president and Congress maintained regular communication, fostering transparency and accountability in the federal government. However, the Constitution does not specify how the president should deliver this information, leaving room for interpretation.

History and Tradition

Traditionally, the Address is given in person, with the president speaking before a joint session of Congress in the Capitol Building in Washington, D.C. The Address became a platform for announcing major policy initiatives, such as President Franklin D. Roosevelt's "Four Freedoms" during World War II. The average speech lasts one hour, although Richard Nixon's 1972 State of the Union speech lasted just twenty-eight minutes.

The annual speech serves as an opportunity for the president to inform the nation about the current state of affairs, outline their legislative agenda, and address key issues affecting the country such as foreign policy, healthcare, education, and the economy.

The very first State of the Union Address was delivered by George Washington in 1790 at Federal Hall in New York City. At that time, New York City served as the temporary capital of the United States.

Back then, the speech was called the "Annual Message" because the president would present his message to Congress, sharing vital information about the country's progress and challenges. Washington believed it was crucial to keep the nation informed about the government's work.

In 1801, Thomas Jefferson changed the tradition and instead delivered a written message to Congress. Jefferson believed that delivering the address in person resembled the British monarch's "Speech from the Throne." It reminded him too much of the way kings and queens did things. Jefferson's new tradition of delivering the State of the Union Address in writing lasted more than one hundred years.

A Return to Speaking

In 1913, President Woodrow Wilson gave the speech in person to create support of the president's agenda. Wilson believed it allowed him to communicate more effectively with both lawmakers and the public. Since then, most presidents have given the speech in person.

Calvin Coolidge, America's 30th president, made history with his State of the Union Address in 1923 by becoming the first president to have his annual address broadcast on the radio. The broadcast allowed Americans from coast to coast to hear the president's words directly, reaching a national audience beyond the walls of Congress.

In 1934, President Franklin Roosevelt (America's 32nd president) officially referred to the annual address given by the president to Congress as the "State of the Union" in his opening remarks. This declaration solidified the name and established it as the accepted title for the speech.

On January 15, 1947, President Harry S. Truman made history as the first president to have his State of the Union Address televised. The televised State of the Union Address became a major event in American political life. In 2002, President George W. Bush's address became the first to be streamed live on the White House website. While the State of the Union Address showcases the president's leadership, it is essential to have a plan in case of unforeseen circumstances.

The Line of Succession

According to the 1947 Presidential Succession Act, the line of succession starts with the vice president, who is first in line to assume the presidency. If the vice president is unable to assume the role, the Speaker of the House of Representatives takes precedence. Next in line is the Senate leader (president pro tempore), followed by members of the president's cabinet in a specific order. The tradition of having a designated survivor gained prominence during the Cold War era when concerns about nuclear attacks were high.

The 25th Amendment of the Constitution clarified the process of succession. It states that if the president is unable to fulfill their duties, they can voluntarily transfer power to the vice president temporarily. The 25th Amendment was ratified in 1967.

A designated survivor is a high-ranking government official who is chosen to remain in a secure and undisclosed location during the Address. His or her identity is kept confidential. This is done as a precautionary measure to ensure the continuity of government in the event of a devastating disaster, incident, or attack. The chosen individual is usually a cabinet member who is constitutionally eligible to serve as president.

PARAGRAPH CODE

After reading about the **State of the Union Address**, head back to the reading and number ALL the paragraphs in the reading passage. Then, read each statement below and determine which paragraph **NUMBER** the statement can be found in. Paragraph numbers MAY be used more than one time or not at all. Follow the directions below to reveal the 4-digit code.

A The tradition of having a designated survivor gained prominence during the Cold War era when concerns about nuclear attacks were high.

B The average speech lasts one hour, although Richard Nixon's 1972 State of the Union speech lasted just twenty-eight minutes.

C Back then, the speech was called the "Annual Message" because the president would present his message to Congress.

D Each year, the State of the Union Address typically takes place in late January or early February.

E A designated survivor is a high-ranking government official who is chosen to remain in a secure and undisclosed location during the Address.

F Calvin Coolidge, America's 30th president, made history with his State of the Union Address in 1923.

G In 1913, President Woodrow Wilson gave the speech in person to create support of the president's agenda.

H Jefferson believed that delivering the address in person resembled the British monarch's "Speech from the Throne."

ELIMINATE ALL EVEN-NUMBERED paragraphs that you used as an answer. Record the remaining numbers (in the SAME order in which you recorded them above) in the boxes below.

MYSTERY WORD

After reading about the **State of the Union Address**, determine if each statement below is true or false. Color or shade the boxes of the **TRUE** statements. Next, unscramble the mystery word using the large letters of the **TRUE** statements.

The Presidential Succession Act was passed in 1947. **D**	Nixon's 1972 State of the Union speech lasted just twenty-eight minutes. **E**	Jefferson's tradition of delivering a written address lasted just four years. **K**	The 25th Amendment was ratified in 1967. **A**
The identity of the designated survivor is kept confidential. **G**	The average speech lasts four hours. **B**	The Senate leader is known as the associate justice. **C**	Washington delivered the first State of the Union Address in 1801. **O**
G.W. Bush's speech was the first to be live-streamed from the White House. **N**	The tradition of a designated survivor gained prominence during the Cold War. **S**	John Tyler was the first to have his address broadcast on the radio. **F**	Reagan was the first president to have his State of the Union Address televised. **R**
Franklin Roosevelt was America's 29th president. **M**	Calvin Coolidge was America's 37th president. **L**	The State of the Union Address typically takes place in late June or early July. **P**	Today, the speech is given to Congress in the Capitol Building. **A**

Unscramble the word using the large bold letters of <u>only</u> the **TRUE** statements.

ELECTORAL COLLEGE

The Electoral College is not an actual place, but a process where 538 electors choose the president and vice president of the United States. The Electoral College meets every four years, a few weeks after the presidential election. Established by the Founding Fathers in 1789, the Electoral College cast votes for presidential candidates based on the voters' wishes.

When Americans cast their vote in a presidential election, they are not directly voting for a candidate but for electors who pledge to vote for a particular candidate. These electors then formally cast their vote for president and vice president. To win the election, the presidential candidate must have 270 of the Electoral College votes, just over majority.

Article II

Article II of the Constitution was a way for the Founding Fathers to establish "checks and balances" within the government. First, Article II allowed for states with smaller populations to have equal influence in the election. Second, men (women could not vote back then) may not have had adequate information on the best candidate for president. At the time, many were unaware of government, politics, and elections because they were farmers, lived in rural areas, or could not read or write. The Twelfth Amendment later made some adjustments to the Electoral College system.

Rather than the popular common vote dictating election results, the electors from each state determine the president. The Founding Fathers chose this method so that presidents are not always chosen from the largest states in the Union. For instance, California has fifty-four electors whereas Alaska, Delaware, and Vermont only have three electors each. The number of electors per state is equal to the total number of its congressional representatives (House and Senate). This means states with larger populations have more electoral votes.

Citizens Vote for President

Citizens vote on Election Day which, since 1845, has been the Tuesday after the first Monday in November every four years. In reality, voters are really voting for the electors of the Electoral College who will cast the final votes representing that state. In forty-eight states and Washington, D.C., the candidate who wins the majority of the popular vote in that state receives all of the state's electoral votes in a system known as "winner-takes-all." The only exceptions are Maine and Nebraska, which use a proportional system that splits electoral votes by congressional district.

Electors Vote for President

Each state has electors known as a slate. If your state has two senators and eight members of the House of Representatives, there would be ten electors for that state's slate. There are one hundred senators and four hundred thirty-five representatives plus three D.C. electors, totaling 538 in the Electoral College. The 23rd Amendment allocated three members to the District of Columbia, ratified (approved) in 1961.

After the popular vote is counted, the electors meet in their respective states in December to formally cast their votes for president and vice president. These votes are then sent to Congress for certification. In early January, Congress meets to count and certify the electoral votes. If a candidate has secured at least 270 electoral votes, they are officially declared the president-elect.

Usually, the popular vote and Electoral College vote results in the same presidential candidate, though in a handful of instances, this was not true. In 2016, the popular vote went to Democrat Hilary Clinton, however, the Electoral College results included 306 votes (of the required 270) for Republican Donald Trump.

Electors usually vote the same way as the people who voted for them; they speak for the people. It is rare that an elector goes against the popular vote, though it has happened multiple times since 2019. No elector has ever been prosecuted for not voting as pledged.

Keep the Electoral College?

There is some controversy on keeping versus abolishing (getting rid of) the Electoral College. As it stands, the Electoral College process protects states' rights. Likewise, keeping the Electoral College keeps the states with larger populations from deciding the vote. Without the Electoral College, states like California and Texas could choose the president each and every time.

Some argue that we need to eliminate the Electoral College because the popular vote may not dictate the winner as in these elections – 1800, 1824, 1876, 2000, and 2016. Another reason, some may give, against the Electoral College is the focus on swing states (states that change their Republican or Democratic tendency). Swing states, also known as "battleground states," may change over time, but in the 2020 election included Arizona, Georgia, Michigan, Pennsylvania, and Wisconsin.

MYSTERY MATCH

After reading about the **Electoral College**, draw a line from the left-hand column to make a match in the right-hand column. Your line should go through **ONE** letter. When you complete all the matches, use the letters with a line THROUGH them to unscramble a mystery word. You MUST start and end your line at the **arrow points**.

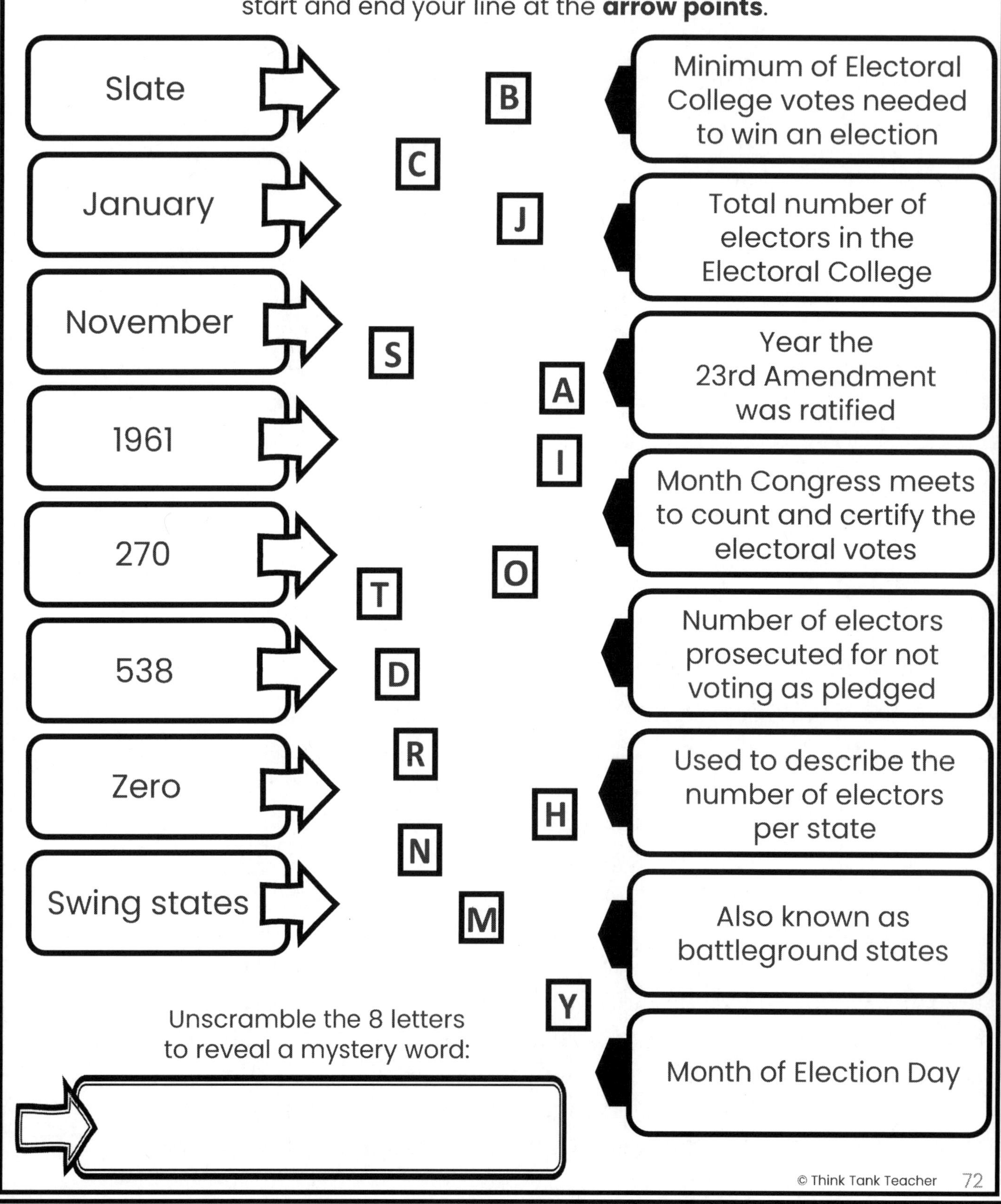

Unscramble the 8 letters to reveal a mystery word:

MULTIPLE CHOICE

After reading about the **Electoral College**, answer each multiple-choice question below. Then, count the number of times you used each letter as an answer (ABCD) to reveal a 4-digit code. Letters may be used more than once or not at all. If a letter option is not used, put a zero in that box.

1 Since 1845, what day of the week does Election Day always fall on?

A. Monday
B. Tuesday
C. Saturday
D. Sunday

2 Which of the following was not a swing state in the 2020 election?

A. Arizona
B. California
C. Michigan
D. Pennsylvania

3 During which election did the popular vote not dictate the winner in the election?

A. 1824
B. 1876
C. 2016
D. All of the above

4 When was the Electoral College established by the Founding Fathers?

A. 1776
B. 1789
C. 1800
D. None of the above

5 Which state only has three electors?

A. Vermont
B. Alaska
C. Delaware
D. All of the above

6 Which amendment allocated three members to the District of Columbia?

A. 4th Amendment
B. 13th Amendment
C. 23rd Amendment
D. 26th Amendment

7 What is the slate of a state with 2 senators and 5 representatives?

A. 2
B. 5
C. 7
D. 10

8 What minimum number of Electoral College votes is needed to win an election?

A. 100
B. 270
C. 435
D. 538

Count how many times you used each letter as a correct answer (ABCD) to determine the 4-digit code. Record your answer in the boxes below.

# of A's	# of B's	# of C's	# of D's

POLITICAL PARTIES

The United States is known for its long-standing two-party system, where two major political parties - the Democratic Party and the Republican Party - dominate the political landscape. These parties are the primary contenders in elections at the federal, state, and local levels, and they consistently win the vast majority of elected offices.

A political party is a group of people who share the same political beliefs. Although there are two main parties, voters may identify themselves as Independent or Third Party. While smaller parties, such as the Libertarian Party or the Green Party, do exist in the U.S., the two-party system tends to limit their influence due to the country's winner-takes-all electoral structure.

The views from different political parties on specific topics are just views, not rules. They are general principles or ideas that not everyone may agree with. Democrats do not have to vote for Democrats, and Republicans do not have to vote for Republicans. Voting has to do with what is going on in the world and your opinion of the candidate and the issues. Political preferences may even vary within a family. The basic disagreement among Democrats and Republicans is the role of the government.

Federalists and Democratic-Republicans

Federalists (led by Alexander Hamilton) supported a strong central government and a loose interpretation of the Constitution. They appealed to merchants, urban areas, and the wealthy elite. This party held power from 1789 to 1801.

Democratic-Republicans (led by Thomas Jefferson and James Madison) supported states' rights, a limited central government, and a strict interpretation of the Constitution.

These early divisions laid the groundwork for the U.S. political system, but the Federalist Party eventually dissolved (disappeared) after the War of 1812. This left the Democratic-Republicans as the dominant political force, where party competition was minimal.

Democrats are often referred to as "liberals." The symbol of the Democratic Party is the donkey, introduced by cartoonist Thomas Nast in 1870. Republicans are often referred to as "conservatives." The Republican Party symbol is the elephant. The Republican Party is also called the GOP or Grand Old Party.

The Birth of the Democratic Party

The modern Democratic Party began a Democratic-Republican split in the 1820s. Andrew Jackson and his supporters broke away to form what is now considered the Democratic Party in 1828. Jackson's followers believed in a strong presidency, support for the "common man," and westward expansion. They opposed (were against) institutions like the national bank, which they viewed as benefiting the elite at the expense of ordinary citizens.

Jackson's presidency (1829–1837) solidified the Democratic Party's reputation. Jackson served as America's seventh president. Democrats of this era supported limited government and individual liberty. In 1834, the Whig Party formed in response to Jackson's view of the National Bank.

The Rise of the Republican Party

The Republican Party emerged in the 1850s in response to the issue of slavery. Founded in 1854 by anti-slavery activists and former members of the Whig Party, the Republican Party's primary mission was to oppose the expansion of slavery into new U.S. territories.

In 1860, Abraham Lincoln became the first Republican president. Lincoln was America's sixteenth president. His election sparked the Civil War (1861–1865) as Southern states, fearing the end of slavery, seceded (withdrew) from the Union. After the Civil War, the Republican Party became associated with Reconstruction and efforts to protect the rights of formerly enslaved persons. As Reconstruction ended, the party's focus shifted toward promoting industrialization, business interests, and economic growth.

The Ideological Divide Today

Today, the ideological divide between the two major parties is more evident than ever, with Democrats and Republicans differing on a wide range of issues, including the role of government, economic policy, healthcare, and social issues.

Democrats generally support a more active government role in addressing economic inequality, providing healthcare, and promoting social justice. The party has strong support from minorities, women, younger voters, and urban populations. Issues like climate change and immigration reform are central to the party's platform.

Republicans emphasize limited government, free-market capitalism, lower taxes, and individual responsibility. The party is supported by rural voters, white working-class Americans, and social conservatives. Key issues for Republicans include gun rights, border security, and traditional family values.

TRUE OR FALSE

After reading about **Political Parties**, read each statement below and determine if it is true or false. If the statement is true, color the coin that corresponds with that question. If the statement is false, cross out that coin value. When you are finished, add the TOTAL of **ALL TRUE** coin values to reveal a 4-digit code. One digit of the code has been provided for you. If the total is 625, a 6 would go in the first box, the 2 in the second box and so on.

A. The Federalist Party was led by James Madison.

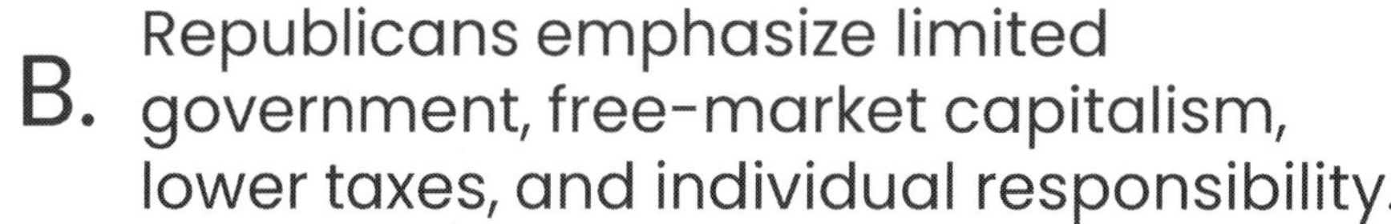

B. Republicans emphasize limited government, free-market capitalism, lower taxes, and individual responsibility.

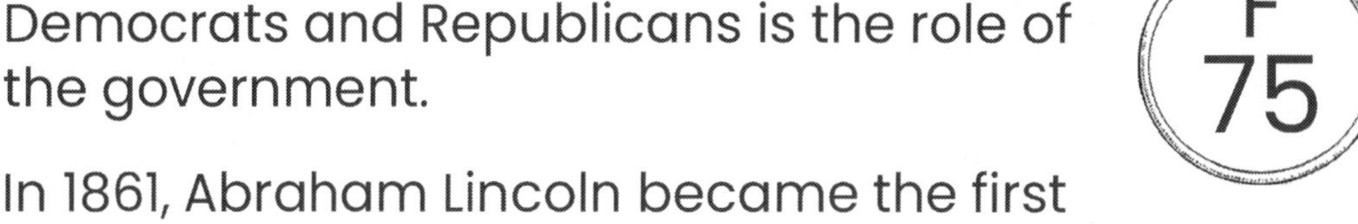

C. The basic disagreement among Democrats and Republicans is the role of the government.

D. In 1861, Abraham Lincoln became the first Democratic president.

E. The Republican Party symbol is the elephant.

F. In 1834, the Whig Party formed in response to Jackson's view of the National Bank.

G. Democrats are often referred to as "conservatives."

H. A political party is a group of people who share the same political beliefs.

After shading the coins based on your answer, add the value of ALL TRUE statements to get the final total. Record your answer in the boxes below.

DOUBLE PUZZLE

After reading about **Political Parties**, determine the word that corresponds with the statements provided below. Spell the corresponding word in the boxes to the right. You may or may not use all squares provided for each answer. Any numerical answers must be spelled out. Next, use the numbers **under** indicated letters to reveal a secret word.

1 Last name of America's seventh president

		7						

2 Democratic-Republicans supported a ___ central government

3								

3 Republican Party symbol

			1					

4 The Republican Party emerged in the 1850s in response to the issue of ___

	9							

5 Last name of person that led the Federalist Party

					5			

6 GOP stands for ___ Old Party

		8						

7 Last name of cartoonist who introduced the Democrat symbol

8 Democrats are often referred to as "___"

	4							

9 The United States is known for its long-standing ___-party system

		2						

10 The ___ Party formed in 1834

		6						

SECRET WORD

1	2	3	4	5	6	7	8	9

ARTICLE III

JUDICIAL BRANCH

The Judicial Branch of the federal (national) government has many jobs, but the most important job is to interpret the laws from Congress. This branch does not make any laws. It is responsible for interpreting what the laws mean and how they legally impact the citizens of the United States. This branch must make sure that the law is not breaking any rules or violating rights listed in the Constitution. The court system is a critical part of checks and balances. This keeps the Judicial Branch from becoming too powerful, while ensuring citizens have basic rights inside of a court system.

Structure of the Judicial Branch

The Judicial Branch, also known as Article III, is made up of courts and judges. The court system in the Judicial Branch is structured in a hierarchy. Each court has a court that is over it or has more authority. The highest court with the highest authority is the Supreme Court. Under the Supreme Court is the Court of Appeals or Appellate Circuit Courts. There are thirteen of these courts. Under the Court of Appeals, there are 94 District Courts.

District Courts

Every state has at least one District Court. District Courts are trial courts where a judge and jury determine guilt or innocence. District Courts hear both civil and criminal trials. These courts have original jurisdiction over most federal cases, meaning they hear the case first, before other federal courts. The 94 District Courts are spread out across the country and further organized into 12 larger areas, called "circuits." These circuits represent the Appellate Courts. For example, the district of New Jersey, Pennsylvania and Delaware are grouped together in the "3rd Circuit." If a person living in that district wants to appeal a decision made by the District Court, they would write to the 3rd Circuit Court of Appeals. The U.S. Court of Appeals for the Federal Circuit is the 13th Appellate Court.

Court of Appeals

The Court of Appeals review decisions made by the lower District Courts and have appellate jurisdiction. This means they hear the case before the Supreme Court. Appellate courts are not trial courts. These courts consist of three judges but there is no jury, no witnesses and no new evidence is presented. Their job is to review the procedures and the decision from the lower District Court and determine if the law was applied correctly in the trial court, and if the court proceedings were conducted unfairly.

Supreme Court

The members of the Supreme Court are appointed, or chosen, by the president, then confirmed (approved) by the Senate. This is done as a system of checks and balances. The final vote requires a majority vote from the Senate (51).

The only constitutional requirement to become a Supreme Court justice is "good behavior." There are no age requirements, no citizenship requirements, and no education requirements. These judges are appointed for life for a reason. They can only be removed from office by impeachment, resignation, or death. To impeach means to accuse of misconduct while in office. This is to ensure that the judges are focused on fairness in the trials – not focused on getting reelected.

Mostly, the Supreme Court deals with cases that have been appealed (request a review) in lower courts. Not all appeals will make it to the Supreme Court, though. Cases must first be decided by a federal District Court, a federal Appeals Court, or a state supreme court. In fact, the justices vote on which cases will and will not make it. Four out of nine justices must agree to hear a case. On average, the Supreme Court hears one hundred cases per year.

The only court listed in the U.S. Constitution is the Supreme Court, giving Congress the power to create lower courts. While the Constitution does not explicitly state how many Supreme Court justices there should be, it is usually between six and nine. Since 1869, the Supreme Court has maintained nine justices. There is one Chief Justice and eight Associate Justices. There are an odd number of justices to prevent a tie decision. Since the 1800s, justices have worn a black robe as tradition.

The judicial process helps ensure that every person has a fair trial with an honest, competent (qualified) judge. The Constitution states that it is a basic right to have a speedy trial (6th Amendment), legal representation, and protection from cruel punishments (8th Amendment). It also states that a person cannot be tried for the same crime twice, called double jeopardy (5th Amendment).

Once arrested, a person will appear before a judge and is legally appointed a lawyer. If the outcome of the trial does not appear fair, it can be appealed. Then, it will go to a higher court. It could potentially go all the way up to the Supreme Court. A decision made at the Supreme Court is final.

PARAGRAPH CODE

After reading about the **Judicial Branch**, head back to the reading and number ALL the paragraphs in the reading passage. Then, read each statement below and determine which paragraph **NUMBER** the statement can be found in. Paragraph numbers MAY be used more than one time or not at all. Follow the directions below to reveal the 4-digit code.

A These courts consist of three judges but there is no jury, no witnesses and no new evidence is presented.

B The only constitutional requirement to become a Supreme Court justice is "good behavior."

C The 94 District Courts are spread out across the country and further organized into 12 larger areas, called "circuits."

D The court system in the Judicial Branch is structured in a hierarchy.

E The only court listed in the U.S. Constitution is the Supreme Court, giving Congress the power to create lower courts.

F The judicial process helps ensure that every person has a fair trial with an honest, competent (qualified) judge.

G District Courts are trial courts where a judge and jury determine guilt or innocence.

H The members of the Supreme Court are appointed, or chosen, by the president, then confirmed by the Senate.

ELIMINATE ALL EVEN-NUMBERED paragraphs that you used as an answer. Record the remaining numbers (in the SAME order in which you recorded them above) in the boxes below.

MYSTERY WORD

After reading about the **Judicial Branch**, determine if each statement below is true or false. Color or shade the boxes of the **TRUE** statements. Next, unscramble the mystery word using the large letters of the **TRUE** statements.

Under the Court of Appeals, there are 124 District Courts. **H**	Supreme Court justices serve a twelve-year term. **L**	Members of the Supreme Court are elected by the people. **F**	The 6th Amendment includes the right to a speedy trial. **S**
There are an odd number of justices to prevent a tie decision. **S**	Not all appeals will make it to the Supreme Court. **I**	To impeach means to accuse of misconduct while in office. **E**	Some states do not have a District Court. **O**
Eight out of nine Supreme Court justices must agree to hear a case. **D**	The Court of Appeals review decisions made by the lower District Courts. **U**	The Judicial Branch is also known as Article IV. **R**	Since the 1800s, justices have worn a purple robe as tradition. **K**
The highest court with the highest authority is the Supreme Court. **J**	On average, the Supreme Court hears two thousand cases per year. **A**	There are thirteen Appellate Circuit Courts. **C**	Once arrested, a person will appear before a judge and appointed a lawyer. **T**

Unscramble the word using the large bold letters of <u>only</u> the **TRUE** statements.

SUPREME COURT

The Supreme Court, located in Washington D.C., is a large, prominent white building with massive columns out front. The Supreme Court was first founded in 1789 as the Nation's Court. Construction of the Supreme Court building began in 1932. It took three years to complete and cost approximately $9 million. It was made of marble from Vermont, Georgia, Alabama, and Italy.

Justices of the Supreme Court

Judges of the Supreme Court are called justices. There are usually nine justices but there have been as few as six. The head of the justices is called the Chief Justice. The remaining eight justices are called Associate Justices. These justices are appointed (chosen) by the president. However, the Senate must also approve of them with a majority vote (51). This process is called Senate Confirmation.

Justices can serve a life-term in the Supreme Court until retirement, impeachment, or death. A life term allows justices to not worry about 'popularity' and therefore base their court decisions on the law, not winning an election. There are no age requirements, no education requirements, no experience requirements, and no citizenship requirements for justices.

The Supreme Court does not have a jury. After the justices have heard the case, they will deliberate and give an opinion on the case. A majority opinion reflects the views of more than fifty percent of the justices. When a justice disagrees with the decision of the majority, a dissenting opinion is given. Ruth Bader Ginsburg, the second woman to serve on the U.S. Supreme Court, wore her famous dissent necklace to signal when she disagreed with the majority opinion of the Court.

Appeals and the Supreme Court's Role

Mostly, the Supreme Court deals with cases that have been appealed (request a review) in lower courts. An appeal is made if someone believes that their court proceedings were unfair. Not all appeals will make it to the Supreme Court, though. In fact, the justices vote on which cases will and will not make it. Four out of nine justices must agree to hear a case. Some cases go directly to the Supreme Court, but this is extremely rare. Most of these cases involve a case against two different types of government. For example, one state may have a court case against another state for water or river rights.

Complex Decisions and Landmark Cases

The Supreme Court makes sure that laws follow the principles and guidelines outlined in the Constitution. The Supreme Court can claim that a law is unconstitutional and overturn it. It can also overturn a previous decision that was made. This happened during the Civil Rights Movement. In 1896, the Supreme Court allowed segregation in public places, including schools, in the Plessy v. Ferguson case. In 1954, however, the Supreme Court overturned their earlier decision by making it illegal to segregate schools in the Brown v. Board of Education case.

The Supreme Court hears about 150 cases per year, and many are highly publicized because they impact people across the nation. Every Supreme Court session starts with the words "Oyez, Oyez, Oyez," which means to pay attention. The annual court sessions run from the first Monday of October through late June or early July.

The Supreme Court often faces complex decisions. Since this court is the highest court, many controversial cases end up here. The Supreme Court can also review the decisions of Congress and even the president as a system of checks and balances. In 1803, Marbury v. Madison established Judicial Review and the importance of the separation of powers.

Other landmark Supreme Court cases include Tinker v. Des Moines which explored the legal concept of freedom of speech and the 1st Amendment. Gideon v. Wainwright was about the right to counsel or a lawyer (6th Amendment). Miranda v. Arizona was about a person understanding their rights and self-incrimination (5th Amendment). New Jersey v. T.L.O. in 1985 was about school searches (4th Amendment).

Famous Firsts

John Jay was the first Chief Justice of the United States. He was appointed by President George Washington in 1789 and served from 1789 to 1795. Thurgood Marshall was the first Black American to serve on the Supreme Court. He was appointed by President Lyndon B. Johnson in 1967 and served until 1991. Before joining the Court, Marshall was a prominent civil rights lawyer who successfully argued the landmark case Brown v. Board of Education.

Sandra Day O'Connor became the first woman to serve on the Supreme Court when she was appointed by President Ronald Reagan in 1981. She served on the Court until 2006. Sonia Sotomayor became the first Hispanic and Latina Supreme Court justice, appointed by President Obama in 2009.

MYSTERY MATCH

After reading about the **Supreme Court**, draw a line from the left-hand column to make a match in the right-hand column. Your line should go through **ONE** letter. When you complete all the matches, use the letters with a line THROUGH them to unscramble a mystery word. You MUST start and end your line at the **arrow points**.

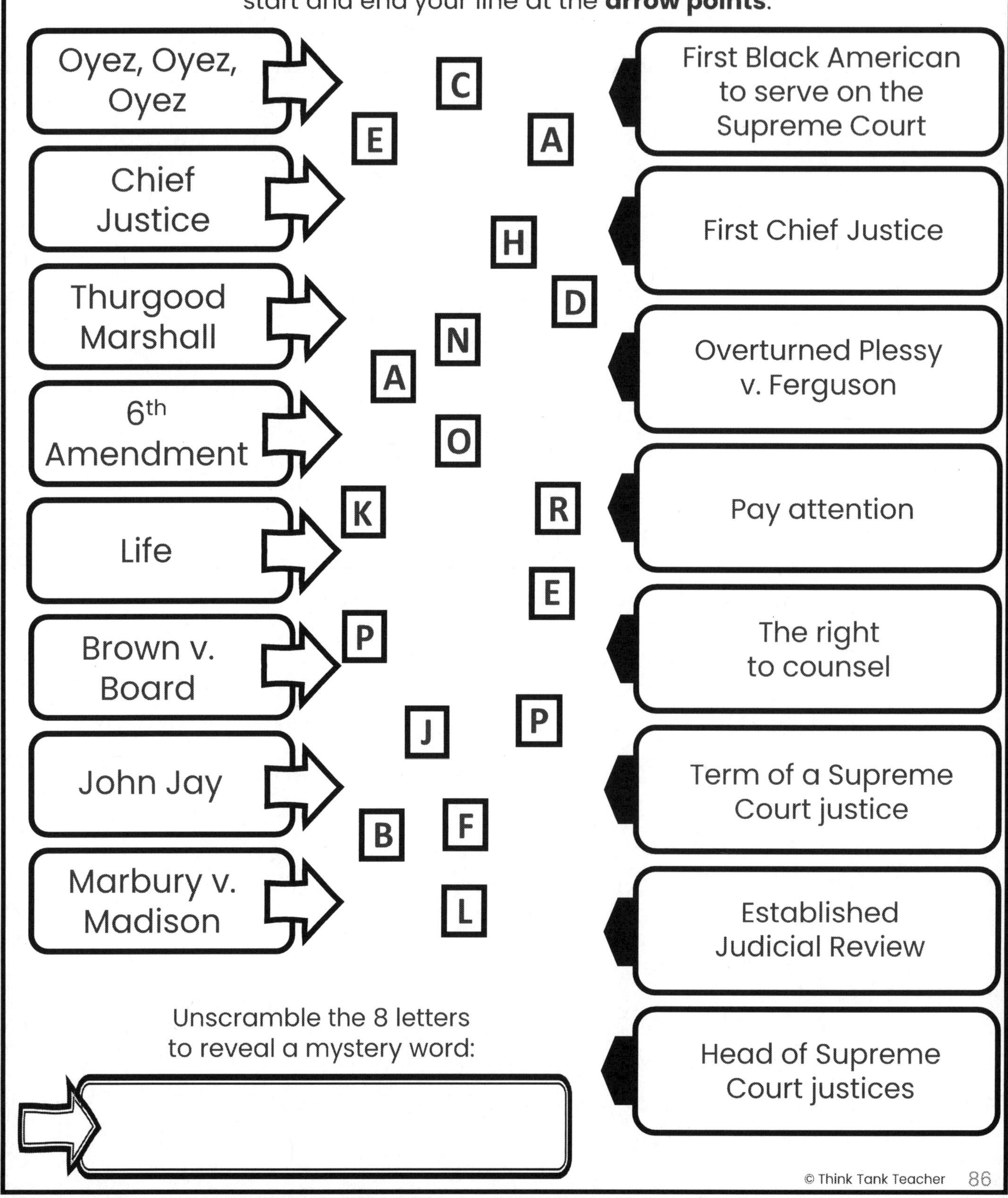

Unscramble the 8 letters to reveal a mystery word:

MULTIPLE CHOICE

After reading about the **Supreme Court**, answer each multiple-choice question below. Then, count the number of times you used each letter as an answer (ABCD) to reveal a 4-digit code. Letters may be used more than once or not at all. If a letter option is not used, put a zero in that box.

1 Justices can serve a life-term in the Supreme Court until which of the following?

A. Impeachment
B. Retirement
C. Death
D. All of the above

2 Who was the first woman to serve on the Supreme Court, appointed by President Ronald Reagan?

A. Sandra Day O'Connor
B. Sonia Sotomayor
C. Ruth Bader Ginsburg
D. None of the above

3 When the Supreme Court was first founded in 1789, what was it known as?

A. 14th Circuit Court
B. The President's Palace
C. The Nation's Court
D. Liberty Building

4 Who famously wore a dissent necklace to signal when she disagreed with the majority?

A. Sandra Day O'Connor
B. Sonia Sotomayor
C. Ruth Bader Ginsburg
D. None of the above

5 Which landmark case was about a person understanding their rights and self-incrimination?

A. Gideon v. Wainwright
B. Plessy v. Ferguson
C. Miranda v. Arizona
D. Tinker v. Des Moines

6 When did Marbury v. Madison establish Judicial Review?

A. 1789
B. 1793
C. 1801
D. 1803

7 Of nine justices, how many must agree to hear a case?

A. Four
B. Five
C. Six
D. Nine

8 When a justice disagrees with the decision of the majority, what opinion is given?

A. Majority opinion
B. Closed opinion
C. Dissenting opinion
D. Circuit opinion

Count how many times you used each letter as a correct answer (ABCD) to determine the 4-digit code. Record your answer in the boxes below.

# of A's	# of B's	# of C's	# of D's

LANDMARK CASES

The U.S. Supreme Court often deals with some of the most challenging legal issues facing the nation. These cases often involve interpretations of the U.S. Constitution and require the justices to carefully consider the balance between individual rights, government powers, and societal values. When the justices make decisions, their rulings set lasting legal precedents, impacting American society for generations. Since they are the final say in legal disputes, they must carefully think through different opinions, legal rules, and how their decisions will impact people and the country.

Plessy v. Ferguson 1896

In Louisiana, the Separate Car Act of 1890 required railroad companies to provide separate but equal train car accommodations for Black and white passengers. Homer Plessy was a Black activist who set out to challenge these laws when he sat in the "whites only" section of a train car. Though he appeared to be white, the conductor asked Plessy of his ancestry, in which he replied that he was one-eighth Black American. The conductor then instructed Plessy to move to the appropriate car. Plessy argued that he was an American citizen who paid for a first-class ticket, and that he would not be moving. Plessy was arrested and fought his case all the way to the Supreme Court. He argued that the state of Louisiana was in violation of the Equal Protection Clause of the 14th Amendment. The Supreme Court ruled segregation (separation based on race) did not violate the Constitution, as long as the buildings or facilities were of "equal standards." The ruling, known as the "separate-but-equal" policy, became the constitutional basis for segregation laws over the next 50 years.

Gideon v. Wainwright 1963

Clarence Gideon was arrested for robbery. Gideon could not afford to hire a lawyer, so he requested that counsel (lawyer) be provided to him by the state. At that time, Florida only provided a lawyer if a person faced the death penalty. Thus, his request was denied. Gideon was sentenced to five years in prison. While in prison, he wrote a letter to the Supreme Court suggesting his 6th Amendment (right to legal counsel) had been violated. He argued that a persons' right to legal counsel should not depend on whether they can afford one. The Supreme Court ruled that the government must provide a lawyer to anyone accused of a felony (a serious crime), regardless of their ability to pay for one. The court believed Gideon's 6th

Amendment was violated, and he was tried again with a lawyer provided by the state. This time, he was acquitted of the crime and released from jail. To be acquitted means to be found innocent. This case ensured rights for those accused of a crime.

Miranda v. Arizona 1966

Ernesto Miranda was arrested for kidnapping and other violent crimes. After his arrest, police interrogated (asked questions) him for two hours and obtained a written confession. Miranda was never informed that he had the "right to remain silent" or that he had the right to a lawyer. In court, the jury found Miranda guilty and sentenced him to 20 years in prison. Miranda fought his case on the grounds that he was not informed of his constitutional rights. He did not know the 5th Amendment gave him the right to remain silent or granted him access to a lawyer during questioning. The Supreme Court ruled in favor of Miranda, claiming he was not properly informed of his constitutional rights. Chief Justice Earl Warren stated, "such safeguards include proof that the suspect was aware of his right to be silent, that any statement he makes may be used against him, that he has the right to have an attorney present, that he has the right to have an attorney appointed to him." As a result of this case, police must read the "Miranda Warning" before questioning a person suspected of committing a crime. The Miranda case led to policy that is still practiced today.

Tinker v. Des Moines 1969

Many Americans were divided over the war efforts in Vietnam. To protest the unpopular Vietnam War, Mary Beth Tinker and her brother wore black armbands to school in Des Moines, Iowa. The students were asked by the school administration to take the bands off, but they refused. Their refusal resulted in a school suspension, so their parents sued the school district. The Tinkers felt their 1st Amendment of Freedom Speech had been violated. Though they were not actively speaking, they were expressing how they felt about the war. Justice Abe Fortas stated that schools "must be able to prove the conduct in question would materially and substantially interfere with the operation of the school." In this case, the school district's actions stemmed from a fear of possible disruption rather than any actual interference. The Supreme Court ruled that these students are citizens and wearing an armband in protest was in fact a form of speech. When the Supreme Court sided with the students, it was a guarantee that all students now and, in the future, had the right to free speech in school as long as the learning process was not disrupted.

TRUE OR FALSE

After reading about **Landmark Cases**, read each statement below and determine if it is true or false. If the statement is true, color the coin that corresponds with that question. If the statement is false, cross out that coin value. When you are finished, add the TOTAL of **ALL TRUE** coin values to reveal a 4-digit code. One digit of the code has been provided for you. If the total is 625, a 6 would go in the first box, the 2 in the second box and so on.

A. Mary Beth Tinker argued that a persons' right to legal counsel should not depend on whether they can afford one.

B. To interrogate means to ask questions.

B
25

C. Plessy argued that the state of Louisiana was in violation of the Equal Protection Clause of the 14th Amendment.

D. The Miranda case led to policy that is still practiced today.

E. The U.S. Supreme Court often deals with some of the most challenging legal issues facing the nation.

F. To protest the unpopular Korean War, the Tinkers wore green armbands to school.

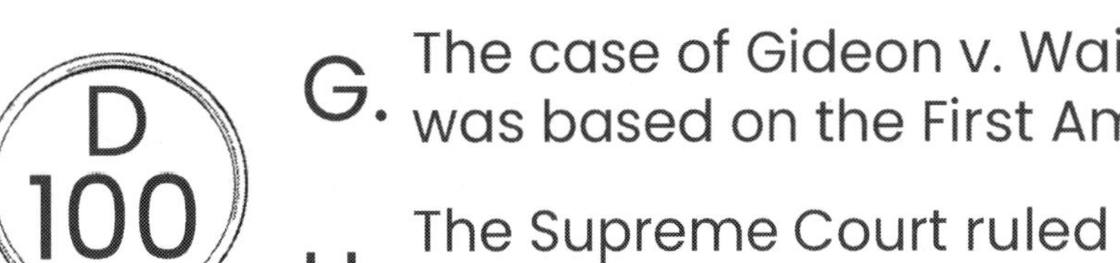

D
100

G. The case of Gideon v. Wainwright in 1963 was based on the First Amendment.

H. The Supreme Court ruled in favor of Miranda, claiming he was not properly informed of his constitutional rights.

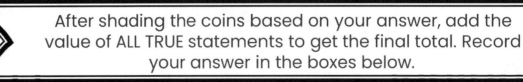

After shading the coins based on your answer, add the value of ALL TRUE statements to get the final total. Record your answer in the boxes below.

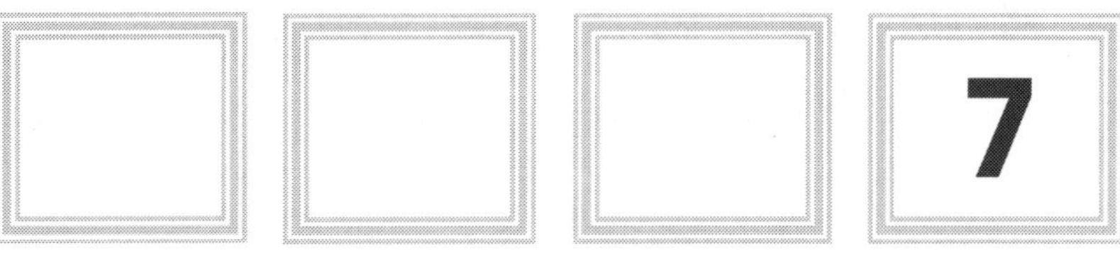

DOUBLE PUZZLE

After reading about **Landmark Cases**, determine the word that corresponds with the statements provided below. Spell the corresponding word in the boxes to the right. You may or may not use all squares provided for each answer. Any numerical answers must be spelled out. Next, use the numbers **under** indicated letters to reveal a secret word.

1	Miranda v. Arizona in 1966 was about the ___ Amendment	☐☐☐☐☐☐☐☐☐ (3 under box 4)
2	Plessy argued this state violated his rights	☐☐☐☐☐☐☐☐☐
3	Last name of the Chief Justice in the Miranda v Arizona case	☐☐☐☐☐☐☐☐☐ (2 under box 6)
4	Synonym for counsel	☐☐☐☐☐☐☐☐☐ (5 under box 6)
5	___ v. Wainwright took place in 1963	☐☐☐☐☐☐☐☐☐ (1 under box 2)
6	Tinker v. Des Moines was about the 1st Amendment and Freedom of ___	☐☐☐☐☐☐☐☐☐ (6 under box 2)
7	To be ___ means to be found innocent	☐☐☐☐☐☐☐☐☐ (9 under box 6)
8	To protest the Vietnam War, the Tinkers wore black ___ to school	☐☐☐☐☐☐☐☐☐ (7 under box 2)
9	Another word for a serious crime	☐☐☐☐☐☐☐☐☐ (4 under box 2)
10	Segregation is separation based on ___	☐☐☐☐☐☐☐☐☐ (8 under box 4)

SECRET WORD

1	2	3	4	5	6	7	8	9

CRIMINAL V CIVIL TRIALS

When it comes to the court system, the role of the Judicial Branch is to ensure justice is administered fairly. There are two types of court cases: civil and criminal. Both cases investigate the violations of a person's rights and determine who is to blame.

Due Process of Law

Due process is the legal requirement that the government must respect all legal rights that are owed to a person. These legal procedures are the administration of justice according to established rules and principles. The 6th Amendment of the Bill of Rights gives citizens the right to legal counsel; the 7th Amendment protects the right to a trial by jury in civil cases; and the 14th Amendment states that nobody shall be deprived of life, liberty, or property without due process of law. The 5th Amendment also establishes numerous legal rights that apply to both civil and criminal proceedings such as double jeopardy.

Civil Cases

Civil cases, or non-criminal cases, are a dispute between two or more parties. A civil case may include contract laws, laws of tort (injured on someone else's property), family laws such as custody or divorce, and employment (job) laws. During the pre-filing stage, both parties may try to negotiate a resolution before any further court action is needed.

A civil case begins when a person files a complaint for a minimum of twenty dollars. To be heard in a federal court, the dispute must be for over $75,000. Roughly ninety percent of all civil cases happen at the state level. The person initiating the lawsuit is known as the plaintiff. The plaintiff, or victim, in a civil case usually sues for monetary "damages." The defendant is the person or party whom the lawsuit has been filed against.

During pre-trial, each side submits documentation. At this time, a deposition may be conducted. A deposition is a formal interview or testimony that takes places in front of a court reporter and attorneys from both sides. A full trial may become unnecessary if a "motion for summary judgement" is filed during pre-trial. This motion is filed when evidence is overwhelmingly leaning to one side ("preponderance of evidence") and the other side likely has no chance to win the case.

Before a trial begins, a jury is selected. Most juries in the United States have twelve members, called jurors. A jury is a panel of unbiased, impartial citizens that have been randomly selected. Lawyers have the opportunity to request dismissal of jurors they think may be biased (leaning heavily towards one side of an issue).

The trial phase begins with "opening statements" from both parties. If necessary, witnesses will be called to the stand and cross-examination will take place. Juries are optional for a civil case and many cases are decided solely by a judge. The outcome of civil cases does not result in the "losing" party serving jail time. Often, the outcomes result in a financial penalty.

Criminal Cases

Criminal trials, though similar to civil trials, differ in regard to the requirements of evidence and punishments. There are two main types of crimes: crimes against people and crimes against property. Crimes against property may include larceny (theft), vandalism, and trespassing. Crimes against people may include assault, homicide, or kidnapping, among other more serious crimes.

A person accused of a crime is generally indicted or formally charged with a crime. An informal hearing takes place to determine if there was enough evidence or "probable cause" to keep the suspect in custody. Probable cause is "a reasonable belief that a crime has been committed." Probable cause can be found in the 4th Amendment of the U.S. Constitution.

During the arraignment, (the first time a defendant makes a court appearance) the suspect is asked to give a plea of guilty or not guilty. The judge will then set bail, directly related to the severity of the crime. The 8th Amendment prevents the judge from setting bail at one million dollars if the crime was stealing a candy bar. With more serious crimes, no bail may be set. Bail is the amount of money paid by the defendant to be released until the trial date.

In a criminal trial, the case is always the Prosecutor v. Defendant. The prosecutor (state attorney) will present the state's case against the person accused of the crime. If a defendant in a criminal case cannot afford a lawyer, one will be appointed to them (6th Amendment).

The defendant is presumed innocent until proven guilty and the state must prove beyond a reasonable doubt (burden of proof) that the jury should find the defendant guilty. The jury will meet in private and reach a verdict. The role of a jury is not to determine guilt or innocence, rather to decide if there is enough evidence to prove a person is guilty of the crime. If the verdict is guilty, sentencing takes place. The sentence may be a fine, imprisonment, or probation, among other punishments.

PARAGRAPH CODE

After reading about **Criminal v Civil Trials**, head back to the reading and number ALL the paragraphs in the reading passage. Then, read each statement below and determine which paragraph **NUMBER** the statement can be found in. Paragraph numbers MAY be used more than one time or not at all. Follow the directions below to reveal the 4-digit code.

A The role of a jury is not to determine guilt or innocence, rather to decide if there is enough evidence to prove a person is guilty of the crime.

B The plaintiff, or victim, in a civil case usually sues for monetary "damages."

C The outcome of civil cases does not result in the "losing" party serving jail time.

D Probable cause can be found in the 4th Amendment of the U.S. Constitution.

E The 8th Amendment prevents the judge from setting bail at one million dollars if the crime was stealing a candy bar.

F Due process is the legal requirement that the government must respect all legal rights that are owed to a person.

G Civil cases, or non-criminal cases, are a dispute between two or more parties.

H A full trial may become unnecessary if a "motion for summary judgement" is filed during pre-trial.

ELIMINATE ALL EVEN-NUMBERED paragraphs that you used as an answer. Record the remaining numbers (in the SAME order in which you recorded them above) in the boxes below.

MYSTERY WORD

After reading about **Criminal v Civil Trials**, determine if each statement below is true or false. Color or shade the boxes of the **TRUE** statements. Next, unscramble the mystery word using the large letters of the **TRUE** statements.

Most juries in the United States have twelve members, called jurors. **D**	The defendant is presumed guilty until proven innocent. **M**	A composition is a formal interview or testimony. **A**	The 9th Amendment protects the right to a trial by jury in civil cases. **H**
Probable cause is "a reasonable belief that a crime has been committed." **N**	A civil case begins when a person files a complaint for at least $1000 dollars. **L**	Juries are optional for a civil case and many cases are decided solely by a judge. **E**	Probable cause can be found in the 12th Amendment. **G**
Laws of tort involve a person injured on someone else's property. **C**	The 6th Amendment gives citizens the right to legal counsel. **E**	If the verdict is guilty, sentencing takes place. **I**	About thirty percent of all civil cases happen at the state level. **R**
The plaintiff is the person or party whom the lawsuit has been filed against. **T**	There are four types of court cases: civil, parliamentary, open and closed. **P**	There are two main types of crimes: against people and against property. **E**	In a criminal trial, the case is always the Prosecutor v. Defendant. **V**

Unscramble the word using the large bold letters of only the **TRUE** statements.

THURGOOD MARSHALL

Thurgood Marshall was the first Black American to serve on the U.S. Supreme Court. Born on July 2, 1908, in Baltimore, Maryland, he played a critical role in shaping civil rights laws in the United States, most famously through his involvement in the landmark case of Brown v. Board of Education. Marshall's legacy stretches through decades of activism, making him one of the most influential figures in the fight for racial equality.

Early Life and Legal Career

Growing up in the racially segregated South, Marshall faced discrimination throughout his life. He attended segregated (separated based on race) schools and later graduated from Lincoln University, a historically Black college. After being denied admission to the University of Maryland Law School due to his race, he attended Howard University School of Law. There he was mentored by Charles Houston, a prominent (well-known) civil rights lawyer.

Marshall became a key leader of the NAACP, serving as its chief counsel. The NAACP was founded in 1909 and formed in response to the violence and discrimination faced by Black Americans. Marshall traveled across the country, fighting for equality in various forms, including housing, employment, and education. His legal work later helped to eliminate Jim Crow laws, the set of state and local laws that enforced racial segregation in the Southern United States.

Brown v. Board of Education

One of Marshall's most significant achievements came in 1954 with the Supreme Court case Brown v. Board of Education of Topeka. In the early 1950s, a group of parents, led by Oliver Brown, sued the Board of Education in Topeka, Kansas. As the lead attorney for the NAACP Legal Defense Fund, Marshall successfully argued that racial segregation in public schools was unconstitutional, violating the Equal Protection Clause of the 14th Amendment. The 14th Amendment, ratified in 1868, guarantees that no state shall "deny to any person within its jurisdiction the equal protection of the laws." At the time, the doctrine (rule) of "separate but equal," established by the Plessy v. Ferguson decision in 1896, allowed for racially segregated facilities as long as they were thought to be “equal”. However, in reality, the facilities provided for Black Americans were far worse than those for white Americans. Schools for Black children were often overcrowded, lacked textbooks and resources, and the buildings were poorly maintained.

Marshall's argument in Brown v. Board of Education focused on the inequality of segregated schools. On May 17, 1954, the Supreme Court, led by Chief Justice Earl Warren, ruled unanimously (100%) that "separate educational facilities are inherently unequal." The decision overturned the ruling of "separate but equal," which had been used to justify racial segregation in public schools for decades. This decision marked a turning point in the civil rights movement, setting the stage for further desegregation efforts across the United States.

The Role of the Amendments in the Civil Rights Movement

Several key amendments to the U.S. Constitution played crucial roles in the civil rights movement, particularly in Marshall's legal battles. The 13th Amendment, ratified in 1865, abolished (got rid of) slavery in the United States. The 14th Amendment, which was central to the Brown v. Board case, provided equal protection under the law to all citizens, regardless of race. The 15th Amendment, ratified in 1870, aimed to protect the voting rights of Black American men by prohibiting (not allowing) racial discrimination in voting.

Despite these amendments, racial discrimination persisted for decades due to local laws, especially in the South. Some states openly defied the court ruling, leading to a series of confrontations, including the famous 1957 crisis at Little Rock Central High School in Arkansas. The National Guard had to be called in to enforce desegregation and escort students to class.

Supreme Court Justice and Legacy

President John F. Kennedy appointed Marshall to the U.S. Court of Appeals in 1961. He served in that role until 1965, when he was selected to be the Solicitor General. As Solicitor General, Marshall represented the federal government in cases argued before the Supreme Court.

In 1967, Thurgood Marshall was appointed to the U.S. Supreme Court by President Lyndon B. Johnson, becoming the first Black American to serve on the nation's highest court. As a justice, Marshall was known for his unwavering support for individual rights and his commitment to ensuring equal justice under the law. He served on the Supreme Court for twenty-four years, from 1967 to 1991. Marshall was also a strong advocate for women's rights and the rights of criminal defendants. Throughout his career, Marshall stood firm in his belief that the law should be used as a tool for social change.

MYSTERY MATCH

After reading about **Thurgood Marshall**, draw a line from the left-hand column to make a match in the right-hand column. Your line should go through **ONE** letter. When you complete all the matches, use the letters with a line THROUGH them to unscramble a mystery word. You MUST start and end your line at the **arrow points**.

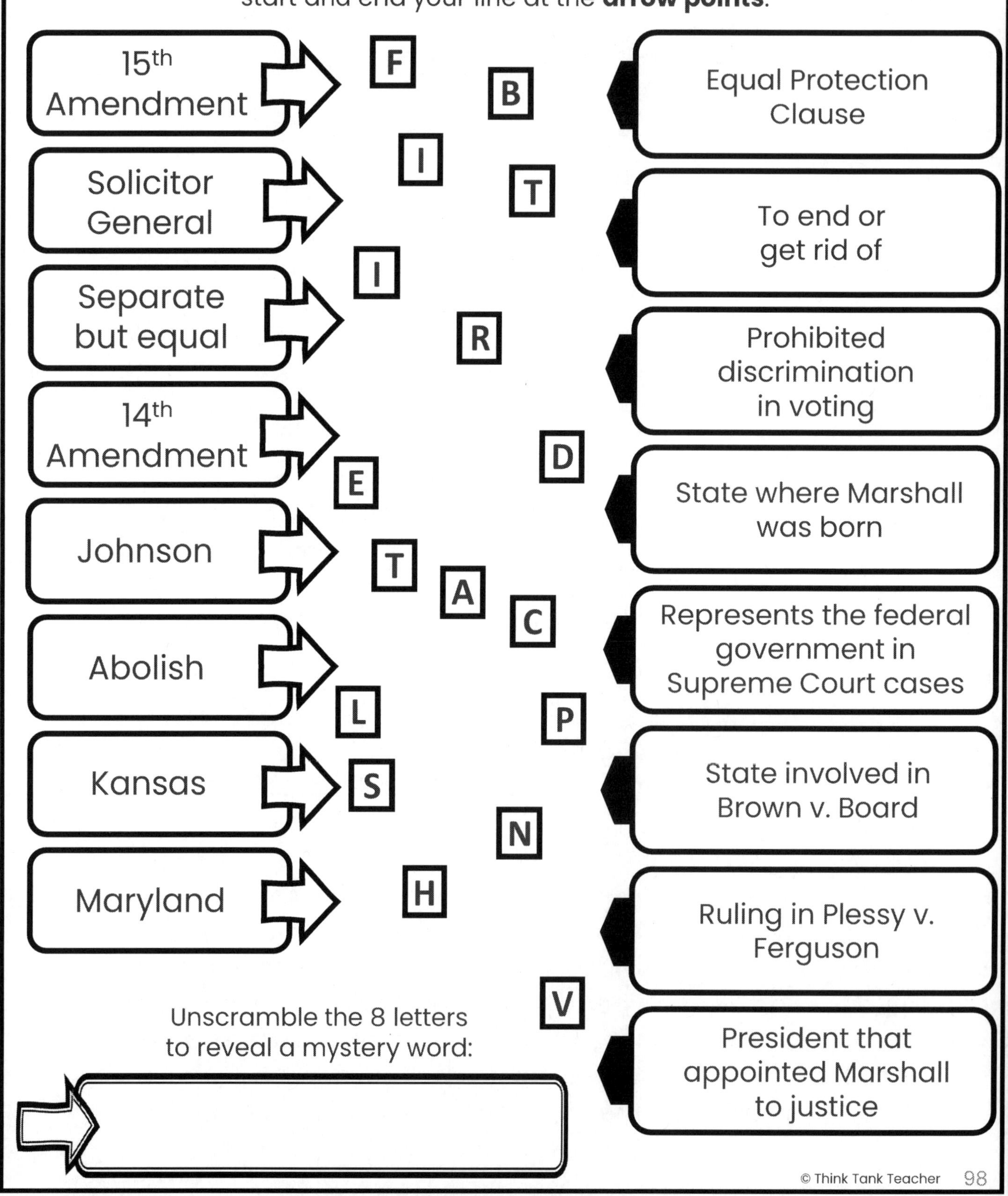

Unscramble the 8 letters to reveal a mystery word:

MULTIPLE CHOICE

After reading about **Thurgood Marshall**, answer each multiple-choice question below. Then, count the number of times you used each letter as an answer (ABCD) to reveal a 4-digit code. Letters may be used more than once or not at all. If a letter option is not used, put a zero in that box.

1 Who served as Chief Justice in the 1954 Brown v. Board case?

A. Thurgood Marshall
B. Earl Warren
C. Charles Houston
D. Lyndon Johnson

2 What clause did Marshall argue was violated in Brown v. Board?

A. Equal Protection Clause
B. Necessary and Proper Clause
C. Establishment Clause
D. None of the above

3 Which amendment abolished slavery?

A. 13th Amendment
B. 14th Amendment
C. 15th Amendment
D. 16th Amendment

4 When was the National Guard called to Little Rock High School to escort students?

A. 1952
B. 1955
C. 1957
D. 1961

5 What law school did Marshall attend?

A. University of Maryland
B. Howard University
C. Topeka University
D. University of Georgia

6 Who appointed Marshall to the U.S. Court of Appeals in 1961?

A. President John F. Kennedy
B. President Herbert Hoover
C. President Lyndon B. Johnson
D. President George W. Bush

7 How long did Marshall serve on the Supreme Court?

A. Fifteen years
B. Seventeen years
C. Twenty-one years
D. Twenty-four years

8 What type of equality did Marshall fight for?

A. Education
B. Housing
C. Employment
D. All of the above

Count how many times you used each letter as a correct answer (ABCD) to determine the 4-digit code. Record your answer in the boxes below.

# of A's	# of B's	# of C's	# of D's

TINKER V. DES MOINES

Tinker v. Des Moines was a landmark Supreme Court case from 1969 that addressed the First Amendment of the U.S. Constitution. The First Amendment, adopted in 1791, includes five freedoms: speech, religion, press, petition, and assembly. The case set an important precedent for students' rights in public schools.

Vietnam War

In the 1960s, America was involved in the Vietnam War, which was an unpopular war with many. The war was fought between North Vietnam and South Vietnam. The North was supported by communist countries such as the Soviet Union, while the South was supported by anti-communist countries including the United States under President Lyndon B. Johnson. Johnson served as America's thirty-sixth president.

In Des Moines, Iowa, in 1965, five students between the ages of thirteen and sixteen decided to express their feelings about the Vietnam War. Among the students were Mary Beth Tinker, her brother John, and their friend Christopher Eckhardt. They chose to wear black armbands as a silent protest against the U.S. involvement in Vietnam. Joined by Christine Singer and Bruce Clark, they planned to wear the black armbands for two weeks.

The Des Moines Independent Community School District found out about their plan. The school district, fearing disruption, quickly adopted a policy prohibiting the wearing of armbands. They also indicated that students wearing armbands would be suspended from school.

In silent protest, the students wore black armbands anyway, with support from their parents. All five students were suspended until they agreed to remove the armbands. After the Christmas break, the students were allowed to return to school, but in another form of silent protest, they wore black clothing for the remainder of the school year.

Tinker's Take Legal Action

The Tinker family believed that their children's First Amendment rights had been violated and decided to take legal action. The families sued the Des Moines school district, arguing that the school district violated the students' constitutional rights of free speech and peaceful protests. While the students did not speak in protest, the armbands represented their position.

The U.S. District Court dismissed the case. The Court considered the school district's actions appropriate and reasonable. Likewise, the Court agreed with the school district's action to maintain school discipline. They argued that the armbands could disrupt learning at school.

The Tinker and Eckhardt families appealed (asked a higher court to review the case) to the U.S. Court of Appeals for the Eighth Circuit. However, the Circuit Court upheld the ruling of the District Court, so nothing changed. The school district won. One more time, the students' families appealed the four-year court battle with Dan Johnston as their attorney. After losing in lower courts, the case eventually reached the United States Supreme Court, backed by the ACLU (American Civil Liberties Union).

Petition for Certiorari

The petition for certiorari was granted by the U.S. Supreme Court in 1968. Certiorari is reexamination of an action of a lower court. The Supreme Court had to consider whether free speech applied to symbolic speech. Tinker's arguments included the 14th Amendment, which includes the "Due Process" and "Equal Protection" clauses. They also argued that armbands were a silent, symbolic form of speech that allowed the students to express their opinions. They claimed that students' free speech did not disrupt learning and expressing ideas is an essential part of education.

The Des Moines school district arguments included the idea that schools are not an appropriate location for protests. Learning with appropriate school subjects is the priority. The Vietnam War was controversial; therefore, this protest could disrupt learning. They indicated that expressing different opinions could lead to bullying and violence. They also claimed that the school only banned armbands, and students were still able to express their opinions in other ways.

Supreme Court Ruling

The U.S. Supreme Court ruled in favor of the students. With a vote of 7-2, the justices ruled that the armbands did not disrupt the learning process at the school. There was no evidence of disruption when the black armbands were worn. In addition, the Court considered the armbands a form of speech since they expressed students' opinions about the war. The Court's majority opinion was delivered by Justice Abe Fortas.

Justice Fortas famously stated that students do not "shed their constitutional rights to freedom of speech or expression at the schoolhouse gate." The ruling emphasized that as long as student expression does not cause a "material and substantial disruption" to the learning environment, it is protected by the Constitution.

TRUE OR FALSE

After reading about **Tinker v. Des Moines**, read each statement below and determine if it is true or false. If the statement is true, color the coin that corresponds with that question. If the statement is false, cross out that coin value. When you are finished, add the TOTAL of **ALL TRUE** coin values to reveal a 4-digit code. One digit of the code has been provided for you. If the total is 625, a 6 would go in the first box, the 2 in the second box and so on.

A. The District Court argued that the armbands could disrupt learning at school.

B. The First Amendment, adopted in 1776, includes seven freedoms.

C. In silent protest, the students wore black armbands anyway, with support from their parents.

D. Appeal means to ask a higher court to review the case.

E. The Supreme Court had to consider if free speech applied to symbolic speech.

F. The Tinker's won the case at the U.S. Court of Appeals for the Eighth Circuit.

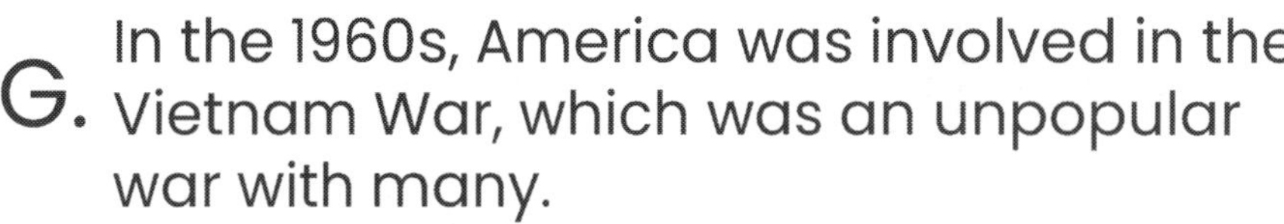

G. In the 1960s, America was involved in the Vietnam War, which was an unpopular war with many.

H. Tinker v. Des Moines was a landmark Supreme Court case from 1974 that addressed the Third Amendment.

D 100

After shading the coins based on your answer, add the value of ALL TRUE statements to get the final total. Record your answer in the boxes below.

DOUBLE PUZZLE

After reading about **Tinker v. Des Moines**, determine the word that corresponds with the statements provided below. Spell the corresponding word in the boxes to the right. You may or may not use all squares provided for each answer. Any numerical answers must be spelled out. Next, use the numbers **under** indicated letters to reveal a secret word.

1	Last name of the justice that delivered the majority opinion		5							
2	In the 1960s, America was involved in the ___ War							3		
3	ACLU stands for American ___ Liberties Union	8								
4	Color of the armbands that students wore in protest	4								
5	___ B. Johnson served as America's thirty-sixth president		2							
6	The 14th Amendment includes the "Due Process" and "___ Protection" clauses					6				
7	Last name of the Tinker's attorney					1				
8	Certiorari is reexamination of an action of a ___ court									
9	The state where Des Moines is located									
10	Number of freedoms included in the First Amendment		7							

SECRET WORD

1	2	3	4	5	6	7	8

MIRANDA V. ARIZONA

The landmark Supreme Court case, Miranda v. Arizona (1966), fundamentally changed how law enforcement interacts with suspects in custody. This case established the now-famous "Miranda Warning," which protects individuals from self-incrimination under the Fifth Amendment and ensures they understand their Sixth Amendment right to legal counsel (lawyer). The case is central to the way the justice system balances law enforcement's duties with the constitutional rights of individuals. The outcome of this case continues to be a cornerstone of American criminal procedure, safeguarding the rights of individuals accused of crimes.

Background of the Case

The case began with Ernesto Miranda, a 23-year-old man arrested in Phoenix, Arizona, in 1963, for robbery, kidnapping, and other violent crimes. The police had little direct evidence linking Miranda to the crime but had suspicions based on circumstantial evidence. After being brought into police custody, Miranda was interrogated (asked questions) for two hours without being informed of his rights to remain silent or to have an attorney present. During the interrogation, he confessed to the crimes, and his confession was used as key evidence in his trial. Based on this confession, Miranda was convicted (found guilty) and sentenced to 20 to 30 years in prison.

Miranda's defense attorneys argued that his confession was unconstitutional because he had not been informed of his rights prior to the interrogation. They claimed that without knowledge of his right to remain silent or his right to an attorney, Miranda's confession should not have been admissible (allowed) in court.

Constitutional Protections

The 5th and 6th Amendments were added to the Bill of Rights on December 15, 1791, when the Bill of Rights was ratified and became part of the U.S. Constitution. The Bill of Rights, which includes the first ten amendments, were introduced to protect individual freedoms and limit government power in order to safeguard citizens' rights in various aspects, particularly in legal proceedings.

The Fifth Amendment plays a crucial role in the Miranda v. Arizona case, particularly in its protection against self-incrimination. The Fifth Amendment states that no person "shall be compelled in any criminal case to be a witness against himself," meaning that individuals have the right to remain silent and not provide testimony or statements that could be used to incriminate (cause to look guilty) them in a crime.

Self-incrimination occurs when an individual provides information or evidence - either verbally or through actions - that directly or indirectly implicates (links) them in a crime. However, there are limitations to this protection. Law enforcement can ask questions related to immediate public safety without reading the Miranda Rights. For example, if police need to find out where a weapon is located to prevent harm, they may ask questions without the suspect invoking the right to remain silent. The Fifth Amendment protects against being compelled to speak or provide written statements but does not apply to physical evidence like fingerprints, DNA, or handwriting samples. For instance, a person can be compelled (forced) to provide their fingerprints without it being considered self-incrimination.

The Supreme Court's Decision

The case was eventually appealed to the United States Supreme Court, where the justices had to decide whether confessions obtained without informing suspects of their rights violated the Fifth Amendment's protection against self-incrimination and the Sixth Amendment's right to counsel.

In a 5-4 decision, the Supreme Court ruled in Miranda's favor. Chief Justice Earl Warren delivered the majority opinion, stating that when individuals are taken into police custody, they must be informed of their rights before any interrogation begins.

Warren stated, "such safeguards include proof that the suspect was aware of his right to be silent, that any statement he makes may be used against him, that he has the right to have an attorney present, that he has the right to have an attorney appointed to him."

These rights, now commonly known as Miranda Rights, became a requirement for law enforcement officers during the arrest process. If these rights are not read to a suspect, any statements or confessions made during interrogation are generally inadmissible (not allowed) in court.

Impact of Miranda v. Arizona

The decision in Miranda v. Arizona was a significant victory for civil liberties, emphasizing the protection of individual rights in the face of government power. It placed limitations on how law enforcement officers could conduct interrogations, ensuring that suspects are aware of their constitutional rights.

PARAGRAPH CODE

After reading about **Miranda v. Arizona**, head back to the reading and number ALL the paragraphs in the reading passage. Then, read each statement below and determine which paragraph **NUMBER** the statement can be found in. Paragraph numbers MAY be used more than one time or not at all. Follow the directions below to reveal the 4-digit code.

A Law enforcement can ask questions related to immediate public safety without reading the Miranda Rights.

B The 5th and 6th Amendments were added to the Bill of Rights on December 15, 1791.

C The landmark Supreme Court case, Miranda v. Arizona (1966), fundamentally changed how law enforcement interacts with suspects in custody.

D The Fifth Amendment states that no person "shall be compelled in any criminal case to be a witness against himself."

E Miranda's defense attorneys argued that his confession was unconstitutional because he had not been informed of his rights prior to the interrogation.

F The police had little direct evidence linking Miranda to the crime but had suspicions based on circumstantial evidence.

G In a 5-4 decision, the Supreme Court ruled in Miranda's favor.

H The case was eventually appealed to the United States Supreme Court.

ELIMINATE ALL EVEN-NUMBERED paragraphs that you used as an answer. Record the remaining numbers (in the SAME order in which you recorded them above) in the boxes below.

MYSTERY WORD

After reading about **Miranda v. Arizona**, determine if each statement below is true or false. Color or shade the boxes of the **TRUE** statements. Next, unscramble the mystery word using the large letters of the **TRUE** statements.

The Ninth Amendment includes the right to legal counsel. **D**	There are limitations to the protection of self-incrimination. **O**	Interrogate means to ask questions. **S**	Justice Earl Warren delivered the majority opinion. **I**
In a 5-4 decision, the Supreme Court ruled in Miranda's favor. **F**	Miranda v. Arizona took place in 1966. **C**	The Bill of Rights was ratified on December 15, 1791. **S**	A person can be compelled to provide their fingerprints. **N**
Ernesto Miranda was arrested in Des Moines, Iowa. **L**	The police had lots of direct evidence linking Miranda to the crime. **A**	Convicted means to be found guilty. **N**	At the time of his arrest, Ernesto Miranda was thirty-seven years old. **R**
The Fifth Amendment does not apply to physical evidence. **S**	Miranda was interrogated for nine hours. **L**	The right to remain silent is now commonly known as Miranda Rights. **E**	To incriminate means to cause a person to look guilty. **O**

Unscramble the word using the large bold letters of only the **TRUE** statements.

UNITED STATES CONSTITUTION

TRUE OR FALSE

After reading about the **U.S. Constitution**, read each statement below and determine if it is true or false. If the statement is true, color the coin that corresponds with that question. If the statement is false, cross out that coin value. When you are finished, add the TOTAL of **ALL TRUE** coin values to reveal a 4-digit code. One digit of the code has been provided for you. If the total is 625, a 6 would go in the first box, the 2 in the second box and so on.

A 75

A. The Preamble begins with the words "We the people."

B. The United States had a document before the Constitution called the Bill of Rights.

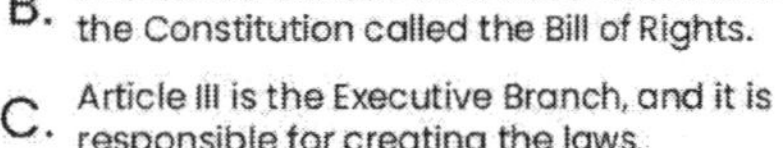

C. Article III is the Executive Branch, and it is responsible for creating the laws.

F 75

D. The U.S. Constitution is a document that states how the federal government should operate.

E. The opening part or introduction of the Constitution is called the Resolution.

F. The 19th Amendment gave women the right to vote.

D 100

G. George Washington became known as the "Father of the Constitution."

H. The Constitution, or plan of government, is organized into ten different parts called Articles.

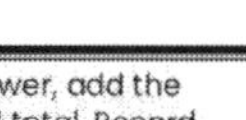

After shading the coins based on your answer, add the value of ALL TRUE statements to get the final total. Record your answer in the boxes below.

2	5	0	2

 1

DOUBLE PUZZLE

After reading about the **U.S. Constitution**, determine the word that corresponds with the statements provided below. Spell the corresponding word in the boxes to the right. You may or may not use all squares provided for each answer. Any numerical answers must be spelled out. Next, use the numbers **under** indicated letters to reveal a secret word.

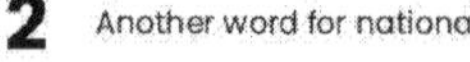
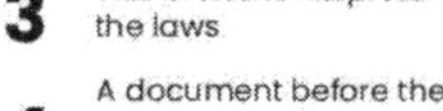
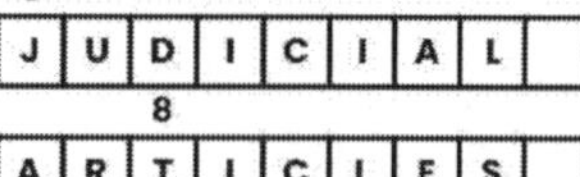
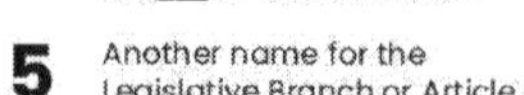
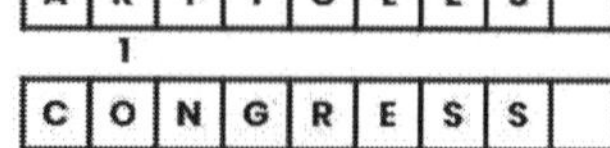
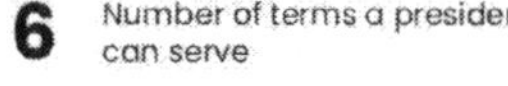
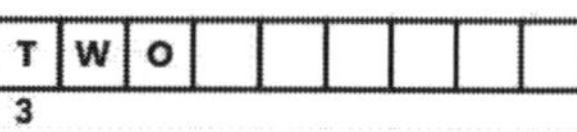
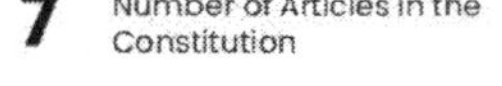
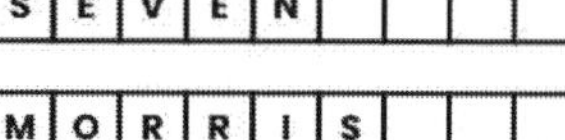
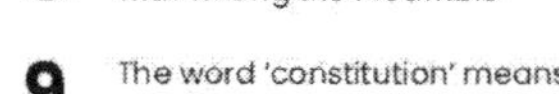
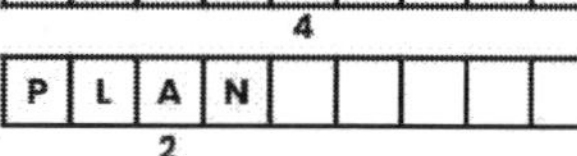
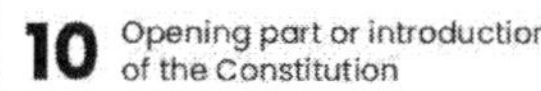

#	Clue	Answer	Number
1	Last name of the oldest delegate to sign the United States Constitution	F R A N K L I N	6 (under I)
2	Another word for national	F E D E R A L	5 (under F)
3	This branch interprets the laws	J U D I C I A L	8 (under D)
4	A document before the Constitution was called the ___ of Confederation.	A R T I C L E S	1 (under R)
5	Another name for the Legislative Branch or Article I	C O N G R E S S	
6	Number of terms a president can serve	T W O	3 (under T)
7	Number of Articles in the Constitution	S E V E N	
8	Last name of person credited with writing the Preamble	M O R R I S	4 (under I)
9	The word 'constitution' means ___ of government	P L A N	2 (under A)
10	Opening part or introduction of the Constitution	P R E A M B L E	7 (under E)

SECRET WORD	R	A	T	I	F	I	E	D
	1	2	3	4	5	6	7	8

 2

BRANCHES OF GOVERNMENT

PARAGRAPH CODE

After reading about the **Branches of Government**, head back to the reading and number ALL the paragraphs in the reading passage. Then, read each statement below and determine which paragraph **NUMBER** the statement can be found in. Paragraph numbers MAY be used more than one time or not at all. Follow the directions below to reveal the 4-digit code.

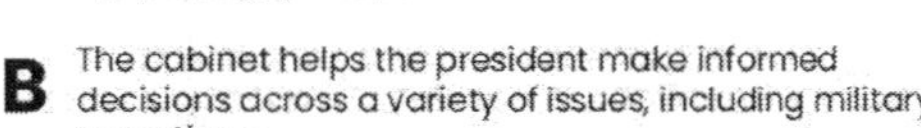
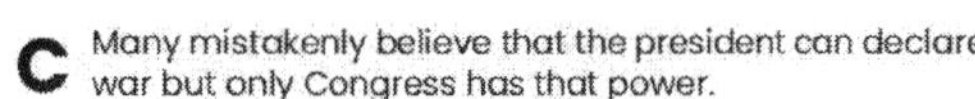
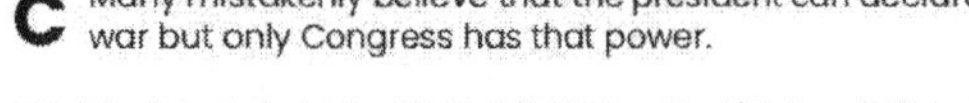
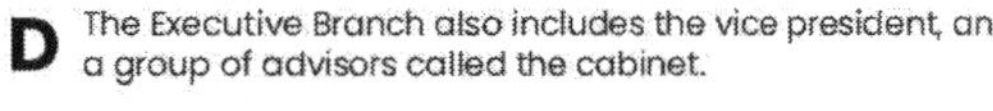

	Statement	Paragraph
A	The Legislative Branch also has non-legislative (non-lawmaking) powers.	5
B	The cabinet helps the president make informed decisions across a variety of issues, including military operations.	8
C	Many mistakenly believe that the president can declare war but only Congress has that power.	9
D	The Executive Branch also includes the vice president, and a group of advisors called the cabinet.	7
E	It can declare acts by Congress and the president illegal and unconstitutional.	10
F	The role of each branch is outlined in the U.S. Constitution in Articles I, II, and III.	2
G	The House of Representatives has four-hundred-thirty-five members and is referred to as the "Lower House."	6
H	With the separation of powers, no branch can infringe on the rights of the people.	3

ELIMINATE ALL EVEN-NUMBERED paragraphs that you used as an answer. Record the remaining numbers (in the SAME order in which you recorded them above) in the boxes below.

5	9	7	3

 3

MYSTERY WORD

After reading about the **Branches of Government**, determine if each statement below is true or false. Color or shade the boxes of the **TRUE** statements. Next, unscramble the mystery word using the large letters of the **TRUE** statements.

U.S. citizens vote for both the president and vice president on election day in November. **D**	The Judicial Branch, Article III, is the federal court system. **E**	Congress can override a presidential veto with a ½ vote. **F**	The Constitutional Convention took place in Boston. **M**
The Legislative Branch can declare war. **T**	Appeals Courts have three judges and do not use a jury. **S**	To impeach means to set aside the punishment for a federal crime. **U**	The main job of the Executive Branch is to interpret the laws. **A**
Each branch has a different purpose and function. **I**	Once the Supreme Court makes a decision, the decision is final. **R**	Together, both the Senate and the House of Representatives are called Congress. **P**	The president is also the Commander-in-Chief of the military. **N**
The president can appoint Supreme Court judges with consent of the Senate. **E**	The Senate has two hundred members and is referred to as the "Lower House." **V**	Supreme Court justices serve a twelve-year term. **B**	Under the Supreme Court are the thirty-six Court of Appeals. **C**

Unscramble the word using the large bold letters of only the **TRUE** statements.

PRESIDENT

 4

CHECKS AND BALANCES

MYSTERY MATCH

After reading about **Checks and Balances**, draw a line from the left-hand column to make a match in the right-hand column. Your line should go through **ONE** letter. When you complete all the matches, use the letters with a line THROUGH them to unscramble a mystery word. You MUST start and end your line at the **arrow points**.

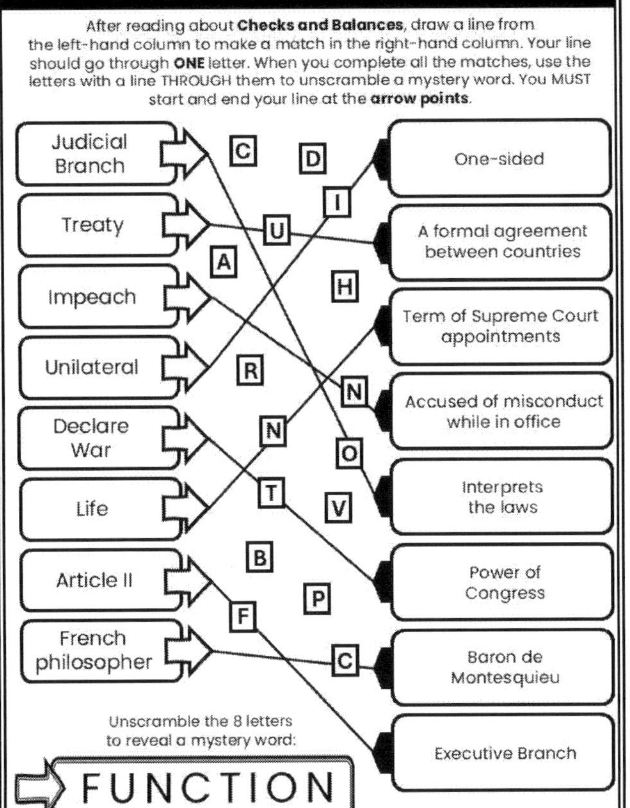

Unscramble the 8 letters to reveal a mystery word:

FUNCTION

MULTIPLE CHOICE

After reading about **Checks and Balances**, answer each multiple-choice question below. Then, count the number of times you used each letter as an answer (ABCD) to reveal a 4-digit code. Letters may be used more than once or not at all. If a letter option is not used, put a zero in that box.

1 What vote is needed in the Senate to ratify a treaty?

A. One-fourth
B. One-half
C. Two-thirds
D. Three-fourths

2 What is the main job of the Legislative Branch?

A. Create the laws
B. Enforce the laws
C. Interpret the laws
D. Veto the laws

3 Which Supreme Court case established judicial review?

A. Bush v Gore
B. Tinker v Des Moines
C. Marbury v. Madison
D. Miranda v Arizona

4 Which of the following is part of the Executive Branch?

A. Cabinet
B. Vice President
C. President
D. All of the above

5 Which part of government must approve of presidential appointments?

A. Senate
B. Vice President
C. House of Representatives
D. Chief Justice

6 The first successful congressional override occurred under which president?

A. John Tyler
B. George Washington
C. John F. Kennedy
D. Franklin D. Roosevelt

7 How many houses is Congress composed of?

A. Two
B. Four
C. Six
D. Eight

8 When was the Constitutional Convention?

A. 1776
B. 1781
C. 1785
D. 1787

Count how many times you used each letter as a correct answer (ABCD) to determine the 4-digit code. Record your answer in the boxes below.

# of A's	# of B's	# of C's	# of D's
4	0	2	2

 6

LEGISLATIVE BRANCH

TRUE OR FALSE

After reading about the **Legislative Branch**, read each statement below and determine if it is true or false. If the statement is true, color the coin that corresponds with that question. If the statement is false, cross out that coin value. When you are finished, add the TOTAL of **ALL TRUE** coin values to reveal a 4-digit code. One digit of the code has been provided for you. If the total is 625, a 6 would go in the first box, the 2 in the second box and so on.

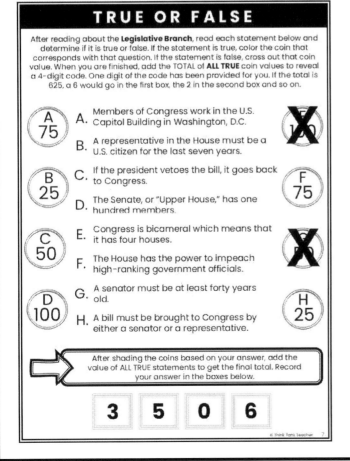

A. Members of Congress work in the U.S. Capitol Building in Washington, D.C.

B. A representative in the House must be a U.S. citizen for the last seven years.

C. If the president vetoes the bill, it goes back to Congress.

D. The Senate, or "Upper House," has one hundred members.

E. Congress is bicameral which means that it has four houses.

F. The House has the power to impeach high-ranking government officials.

G. A senator must be at least forty years old.

H. A bill must be brought to Congress by either a senator or a representative.

Coins: A 75, B 25, C 50, D 100, E 100 (crossed out), F 75, G 50 (crossed out), H 25

After shading the coins based on your answer, add the value of ALL TRUE statements to get the final total. Record your answer in the boxes below.

3	5	0	6

 7

DOUBLE PUZZLE

After reading about the **Legislative Branch**, determine the word that corresponds with the statements provided below. Spell the corresponding word in the boxes to the right. You may or may not use all squares provided for each answer. Any numerical answers must be spelled out. Next, use the numbers **under** indicated letters to reveal a secret word.

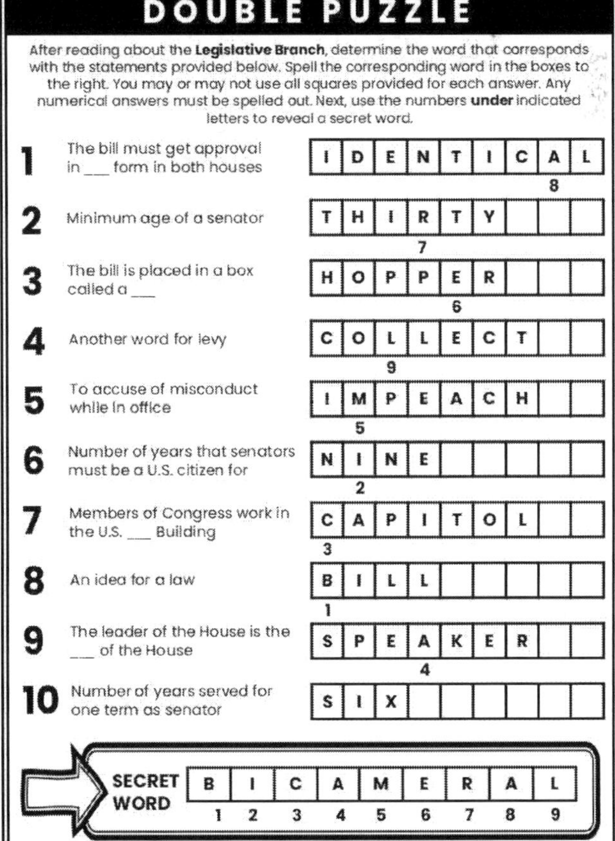

#	Clue	Answer	Number
1	The bill must get approval in ___ form in both houses	IDENTICAL	8
2	Minimum age of a senator	THIRTY	7
3	The bill is placed in a box called a ___	HOPPER	6
4	Another word for levy	COLLECT	9
5	To accuse of misconduct while in office	IMPEACH	5
6	Number of years that senators must be a U.S. citizen for	NINE	2
7	Members of Congress work in the U.S. ___ Building	CAPITOL	3
8	An idea for a law	BILL	1
9	The leader of the House is the ___ of the House	SPEAKER	4
10	Number of years served for one term as senator	SIX	

SECRET WORD

B	I	C	A	M	E	R	A	L
1	2	3	4	5	6	7	8	9

 8

CAPITOL BUILDING

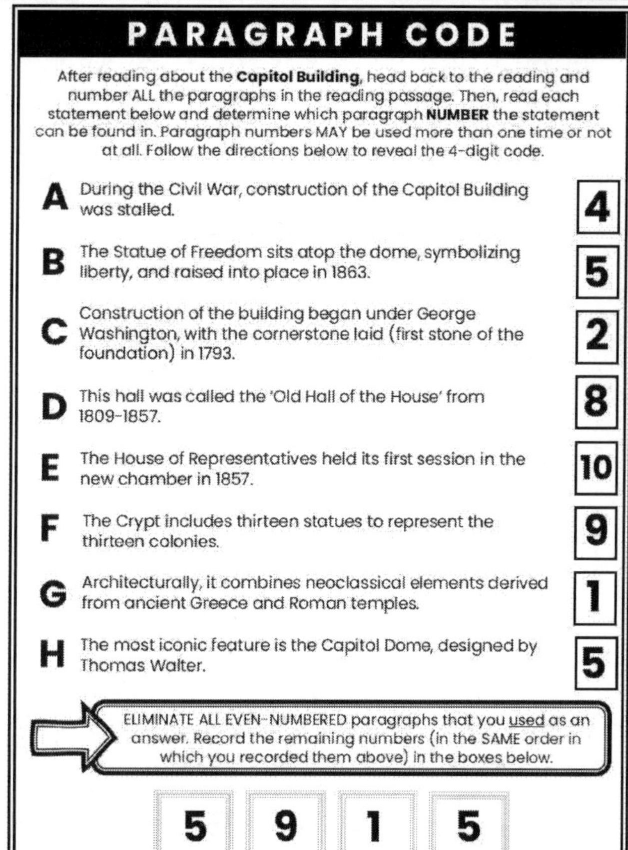

PARAGRAPH CODE

After reading about the **Capitol Building**, head back to the reading and number ALL the paragraphs in the reading passage. Then, read each statement below and determine which paragraph **NUMBER** the statement can be found in. Paragraph numbers MAY be used more than one time or not at all. Follow the directions below to reveal the 4-digit code.

	Statement	#
A	During the Civil War, construction of the Capitol Building was stalled.	4
B	The Statue of Freedom sits atop the dome, symbolizing liberty, and raised into place in 1863.	5
C	Construction of the building began under George Washington, with the cornerstone laid (first stone of the foundation) in 1793.	2
D	This hall was called the 'Old Hall of the House' from 1809-1857.	8
E	The House of Representatives held its first session in the new chamber in 1857.	10
F	The Crypt includes thirteen statues to represent the thirteen colonies.	9
G	Architecturally, it combines neoclassical elements derived from ancient Greece and Roman temples.	1
H	The most iconic feature is the Capitol Dome, designed by Thomas Walter.	5

ELIMINATE ALL EVEN-NUMBERED paragraphs that you used as an answer. Record the remaining numbers (in the SAME order in which you recorded them above) in the boxes below.

5	9	1	5

© Think Tank Teacher 9

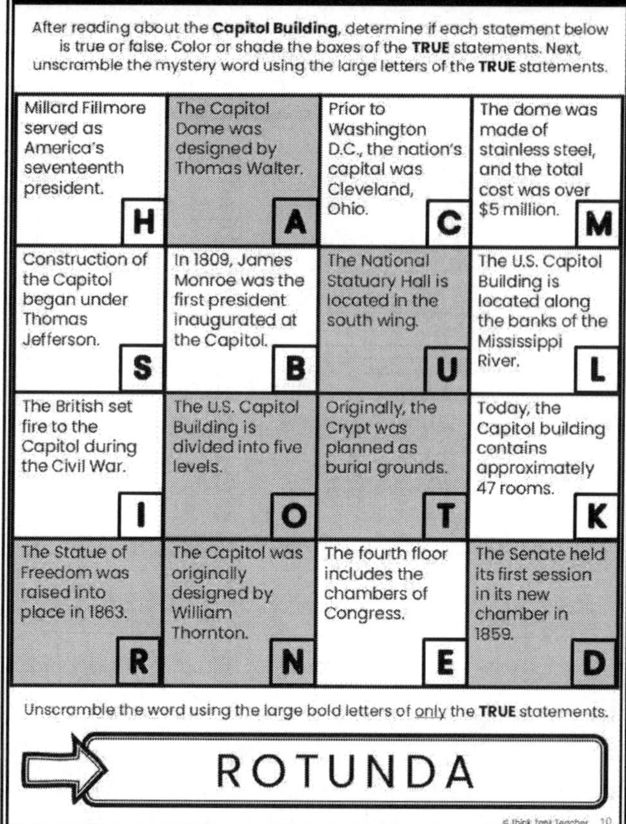

MYSTERY WORD

After reading about the **Capitol Building**, determine if each statement below is true or false. Color or shade the boxes of the **TRUE** statements. Next, unscramble the mystery word using the large letters of the **TRUE** statements.

Millard Fillmore served as America's seventeenth president. **H**	The Capitol Dome was designed by Thomas Walter. **A**	Prior to Washington D.C., the nation's capital was Cleveland, Ohio. **C**	The dome was made of stainless steel, and the total cost was over $5 million. **M**
Construction of the Capitol began under Thomas Jefferson. **S**	In 1809, James Monroe was the first president inaugurated at the Capitol. **B**	The National Statuary Hall is located in the south wing. **U**	The U.S. Capitol Building is located along the banks of the Mississippi River. **L**
The British set fire to the Capitol during the Civil War. **I**	The U.S. Capitol Building is divided into five levels. **O**	Originally, the Crypt was planned as burial grounds. **T**	Today, the Capitol building contains approximately 47 rooms. **K**
The Statue of Freedom was raised into place in 1863. **R**	The Capitol was originally designed by William Thornton. **N**	The fourth floor includes the chambers of Congress. **E**	The Senate held its first session in its new chamber in 1859. **D**

Unscramble the word using the large bold letters of only the **TRUE** statements.

ROTUNDA

© Think Tank Teacher 10

SENATE

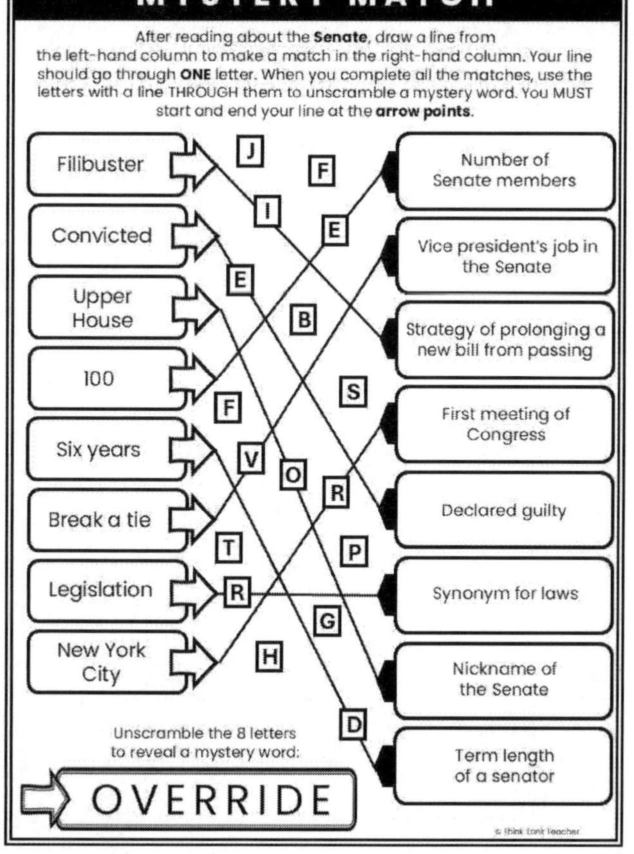

MYSTERY MATCH

After reading about the **Senate**, draw a line from the left-hand column to make a match in the right-hand column. Your line should go through **ONE** letter. When you complete all the matches, use the letters with a line THROUGH them to unscramble a mystery word. You MUST start and end your line at the **arrow points**.

Filibuster
Convicted
Upper House
100
Six years
Break a tie
Legislation
New York City
J
F
I
E
E
B
S
F
V
O
R
T
P
R
G
H
D
Number of Senate members
Vice president's job in the Senate
Strategy of prolonging a new bill from passing
First meeting of Congress
Declared guilty
Synonym for laws
Nickname of the Senate
Term length of a senator

Unscramble the 8 letters to reveal a mystery word:

OVERRIDE

© Think Tank Teacher

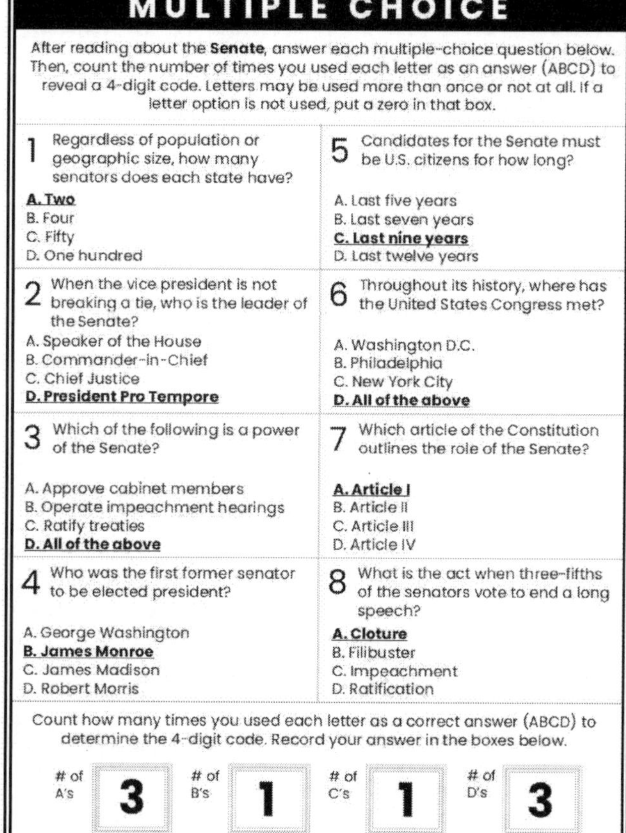

MULTIPLE CHOICE

After reading about the **Senate**, answer each multiple-choice question below. Then, count the number of times you used each letter as an answer (ABCD) to reveal a 4-digit code. Letters may be used more than once or not at all. If a letter option is not used, put a zero in that box.

1 Regardless of population or geographic size, how many senators does each state have?

A. Two
B. Four
C. Fifty
D. One hundred

2 When the vice president is not breaking a tie, who is the leader of the Senate?

A. Speaker of the House
B. Commander-in-Chief
C. Chief Justice
D. President Pro Tempore

3 Which of the following is a power of the Senate?

A. Approve cabinet members
B. Operate impeachment hearings
C. Ratify treaties
D. All of the above

4 Who was the first former senator to be elected president?

A. George Washington
B. James Monroe
C. James Madison
D. Robert Morris

5 Candidates for the Senate must be U.S. citizens for how long?

A. Last five years
B. Last seven years
C. Last nine years
D. Last twelve years

6 Throughout its history, where has the United States Congress met?

A. Washington D.C.
B. Philadelphia
C. New York City
D. All of the above

7 Which article of the Constitution outlines the role of the Senate?

A. Article I
B. Article II
C. Article III
D. Article IV

8 What is the act when three-fifths of the senators vote to end a long speech?

A. Cloture
B. Filibuster
C. Impeachment
D. Ratification

Count how many times you used each letter as a correct answer (ABCD) to determine the 4-digit code. Record your answer in the boxes below.

# of A's	# of B's	# of C's	# of D's
3	1	1	3

© Think Tank Teacher 12

HOUSE OF REPRESENTATIVES

TRUE OR FALSE

After reading about the **House of Representatives**, read each statement below and determine if it is true or false. If the statement is true, color the coin that corresponds with that question. If the statement is false, cross out that coin value. When you are finished, add the TOTAL of **ALL TRUE** coin values to reveal a 4-digit code. One digit of the code has been provided for you. If the total is 625, a 6 would go in the first box, the 2 in the second box and so on.

A 75 / B 25 / C 50 / D 100 / E 100 (crossed out) / F 75 / G 50 / H 25 (crossed out)

A. Once elected, representatives serve a two-year term.

B. A state with a higher population will have a higher number of representatives.

C. Both the House and the Senate must agree to, vote on, and adopt identical bills in order for a bill to become a law.

D. The leader of the House is called the Speaker of the House.

E. Jeannette Rankin became the first woman to serve as Speaker of the House in 2007.

F. The representatives are redistributed in each state every ten years to account for the changing populations.

G. To impeach means to accuse or charge with misconduct while in office.

H. Members elected to the House must be thirty-five years old.

After shading the coins based on your answer, add the value of ALL TRUE statements to get the final total. Record your answer in the boxes below.

3	7	5	0

 13

DOUBLE PUZZLE

After reading about the **House of Representatives**, determine the word that corresponds with the statements provided below. Spell the corresponding word in the boxes to the right. You may or may not use all squares provided for each answer. Any numerical answers must be spelled out. Next, use the numbers **under** indicated letters to reveal a secret word.

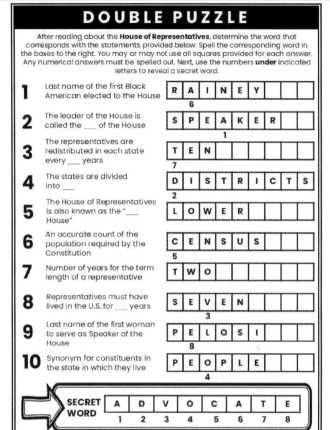

#	Statement	Answer	Number
1	Last name of the first Black American elected to the House	RAINEY	6 (under R)
2	The leader of the House is called the ___ of the House	SPEAKER	1 (under A)
3	The representatives are redistributed in each state every ___ years	TEN	7 (under T)
4	The states are divided into ___	DISTRICTS	2 (under D)
5	The House of Representatives is also known as the "___ House"	LOWER	
6	An accurate count of the population required by the Constitution	CENSUS	5 (under C)
7	Number of years for the term length of a representative	TWO	
8	Representatives must have lived in the U.S. for ___ years	SEVEN	3 (under V)
9	Last name of the first woman to serve as Speaker of the House	PELOSI	8 (under E)
10	Synonym for constituents in the state in which they live	PEOPLE	4 (under O)

SECRET WORD

A	D	V	O	C	A	T	E
1	2	3	4	5	6	7	8

 14

FROM BILL TO LAW

PARAGRAPH CODE

After reading about **Bill to Law**, head back to the reading and number ALL the paragraphs in the reading passage. Then, read each statement below and determine which paragraph **NUMBER** the statement can be found in. Paragraph numbers MAY be used more than one time or not at all. Follow the directions below to reveal the 4-digit code.

	Statement	Paragraph
A	Both the House and the Senate must pass the exact same version of the bill.	8
B	If the bill is not approved by the committee, it often "dies" there and goes no further.	5
C	The sponsor places the bill in a wooden box next to the clerk's desk called the "hopper."	3
D	Once a bill has been drafted, the sponsor introduces the bill to the floor of the House or Senate.	3
E	Washington vetoed a bill regarding the apportionment (distribution) of seats in the House of Representatives.	12
F	If enough senators (three-fifths) agree to cloture, it means the talking must end, and the Senate can move forward with voting on the bill.	10
G	Congress, the president, and even outside groups or people (constituents) can draft (write) a bill.	2
H	The Senate can stall the bill at this point by delivering a lengthy speech called a filibuster.	9

ELIMINATE ALL EVEN-NUMBERED paragraphs that you used as an answer. Record the remaining numbers (in the SAME order in which you recorded them above) in the boxes below.

5	3	3	9

 15

MYSTERY WORD

After reading about **Bill to Law**, determine if each statement below is true or false. Color or shade the boxes of the **TRUE** statements. Next, unscramble the mystery word using the large letters of the **TRUE** statements.

Only fourteen percent of bills "die" in committee. **H**	Cloture requires a one-third vote in the House. **P**	Bills about money must begin in the House of Representatives. **T**	A cloture motion of the Senate would be needed to stop the filibuster. **M**
If two-thirds of both houses vote to override the veto, it becomes a law. **T**	The Civil Rights Act of 1866 was vetoed by President Abraham Lincoln. **D**	Johnson was America's seventeenth president. **M**	Committees can amend the bill by suggesting changes to the bill. **E**
The Rules Committee determines the date for the debate. **I**	The president has twenty days to sign a bill into law. **N**	The first bill vetoed by a U.S. President was in 1792. **O**	Conference committees include members from the both houses. **E**
Today, the filibuster is frequently used. **A**	Strom Thurmond filibustered the Civil Rights Act of 1957 for six days. **S**	Any person can formally introduce and sponsor a bill. **B**	The first bill introduced in Congress was on May 19, 1789. **C**

Unscramble the word using the large bold letters of only the **TRUE** statements.

COMMITTEE

 16

POWERS OF CONGRESS

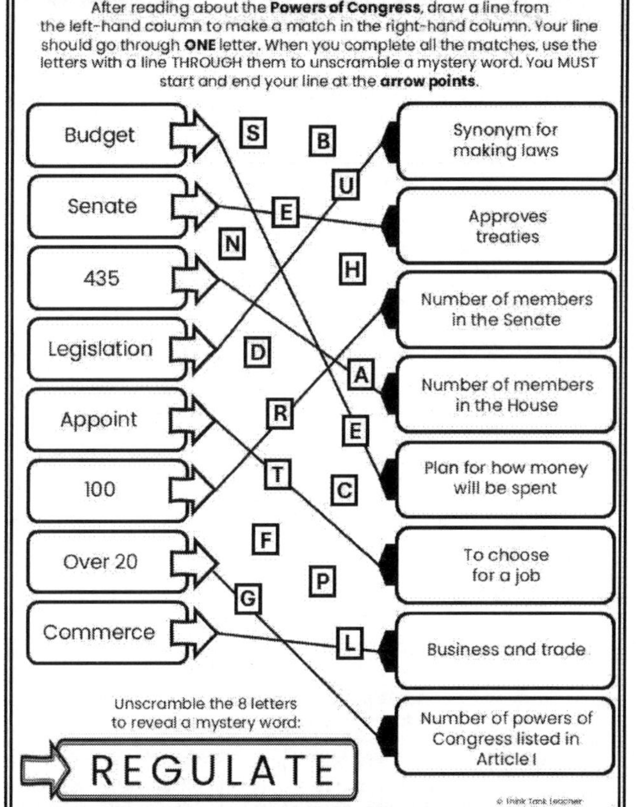

MYSTERY MATCH

After reading about the **Powers of Congress**, draw a line from the left-hand column to make a match in the right-hand column. Your line should go through **ONE** letter. When you complete all the matches, use the letters with a line THROUGH them to unscramble a mystery word. You MUST start and end your line at the **arrow points**.

Budget	Synonym for making laws
Senate	Approves treaties
435	Number of members in the Senate
Legislation	Number of members in the House
Appoint	Plan for how money will be spent
100	To choose for a job
Over 20	Business and trade
Commerce	Number of powers of Congress listed in Article I

Letters: S B U E N H D A R E T C F P G L

Unscramble the 8 letters to reveal a mystery word:

REGULATE

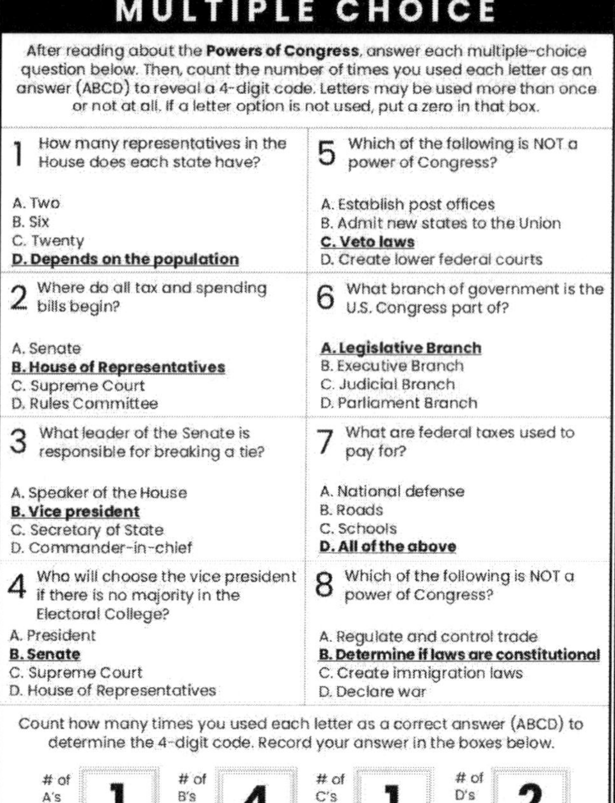

MULTIPLE CHOICE

After reading about the **Powers of Congress**, answer each multiple-choice question below. Then, count the number of times you used each letter as an answer (ABCD) to reveal a 4-digit code. Letters may be used more than once or not at all. If a letter option is not used, put a zero in that box.

1 How many representatives in the House does each state have?
A. Two
B. Six
C. Twenty
D. Depends on the population

2 Where do all tax and spending bills begin?
A. Senate
B. House of Representatives
C. Supreme Court
D. Rules Committee

3 What leader of the Senate is responsible for breaking a tie?
A. Speaker of the House
B. Vice president
C. Secretary of State
D. Commander-in-chief

4 Who will choose the vice president if there is no majority in the Electoral College?
A. President
B. Senate
C. Supreme Court
D. House of Representatives

5 Which of the following is NOT a power of Congress?
A. Establish post offices
B. Admit new states to the Union
C. Veto laws
D. Create lower federal courts

6 What branch of government is the U.S. Congress part of?
A. Legislative Branch
B. Executive Branch
C. Judicial Branch
D. Parliament Branch

7 What are federal taxes used to pay for?
A. National defense
B. Roads
C. Schools
D. All of the above

8 Which of the following is NOT a power of Congress?
A. Regulate and control trade
B. Determine if laws are constitutional
C. Create immigration laws
D. Declare war

Count how many times you used each letter as a correct answer (ABCD) to determine the 4-digit code. Record your answer in the boxes below.

# of A's	# of B's	# of C's	# of D's
1	4	1	2

EXECUTIVE BRANCH

TRUE OR FALSE

After reading about the **Executive Branch**, read each statement below and determine if it is true or false. If the statement is true, color the coin that corresponds with that question. If the statement is false, cross out that coin value. When you are finished, add the TOTAL of **ALL TRUE** coin values to reveal a 4-digit code. One digit of the code has been provided for you. If the total is 625, a 6 would go in the first box, the 2 in the second box and so on.

A. The vice president is responsible for breaking a tie in the Senate.
B. The president can appoint Supreme Court judges and cabinet members with consent by the Senate.
C. George Washington's cabinet had forty members, so it has shrunk over time.
D. The U.S. Constitution includes five requirements to become president.
E. If the vice president is unable to take on the role of president, the Secretary of Defense is next in line.
F. The 24th Amendment prevented any one president from serving more than two consecutive terms.
G. The position of the president is limited to a maximum of four six-year terms.
H. The cabinet is a group of advisors that specialize in certain areas like education or defense.

Coins: A 75, B 25, H 25 (others crossed out: X)

After shading the coins based on your answer, add the value of ALL TRUE statements to get the final total. Record your answer in the boxes below.

1	2	5	2

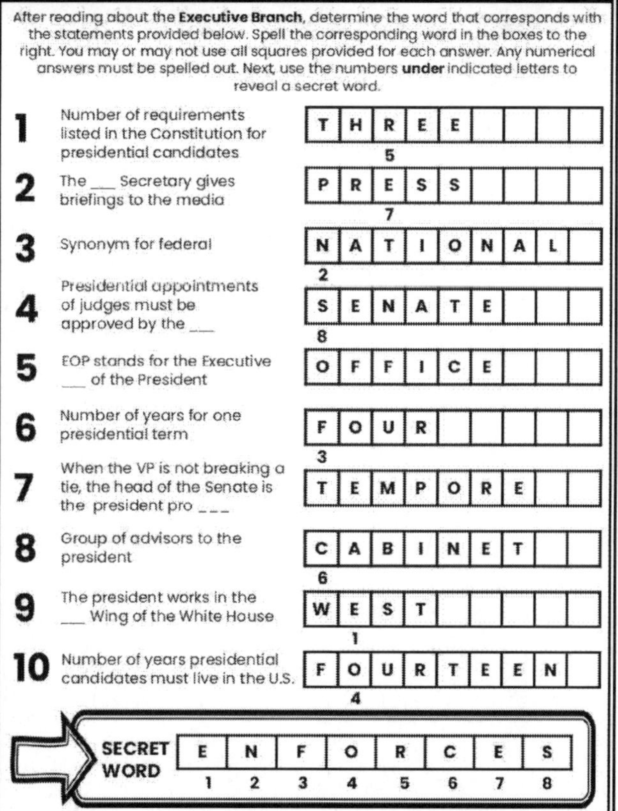

DOUBLE PUZZLE

After reading about the **Executive Branch**, determine the word that corresponds with the statements provided below. Spell the corresponding word in the boxes to the right. You may or may not use all squares provided for each answer. Any numerical answers must be spelled out. Next, use the numbers **under** indicated letters to reveal a secret word.

#	Statement	Answer	Number
1	Number of requirements listed in the Constitution for presidential candidates	THREE	5
2	The ___ Secretary gives briefings to the media	PRESS	7
3	Synonym for federal	NATIONAL	2
4	Presidential appointments of judges must be approved by the ___	SENATE	8
5	EOP stands for the Executive ___ of the President	OFFICE	
6	Number of years for one presidential term	FOUR	3
7	When the VP is not breaking a tie, the head of the Senate is the president pro ___	TEMPORE	
8	Group of advisors to the president	CABINET	6
9	The president works in the ___ Wing of the White House	WEST	1
10	Number of years presidential candidates must live in the U.S.	FOURTEEN	4

SECRET WORD

E	N	F	O	R	C	E	S
1	2	3	4	5	6	7	8

WHITE HOUSE

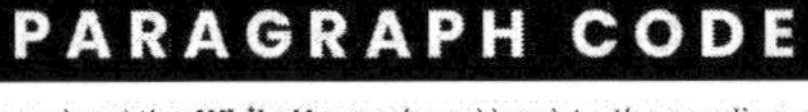

PARAGRAPH CODE

After reading about the **White House**, head back to the reading and number ALL the paragraphs in the reading passage. Then, read each statement below and determine which paragraph **NUMBER** the statement can be found in. Paragraph numbers MAY be used more than one time or not at all. Follow the directions below to reveal the 4-digit code.

	Statement	#
A	First Lady Dolley Madison, wife of President James Madison, famously saved a portrait of George Washington before fleeing.	4
B	The White House sits on eighteen acres of beautifully landscaped grounds, including the South Lawn and the Rose Garden.	10
C	It also contains the State Dining Room, Blue Room, and Red Room, which are used for official events.	9
D	The building has a swimming pool, bowling alley, and a movie theater.	7
E	Construction of the White House began in 1792, after President George Washington selected the site.	2
F	The East Wing contains the offices of the First Lady and is often used for hosting tours and events.	9
G	In 1891, President Benjamin Harrison had electricity added to the house for the first time.	6
H	Originally, the building was called the "President's Palace" or "Executive Mansion."	3

ELIMINATE ALL EVEN-NUMBERED paragraphs that you used as an answer. Record the remaining numbers (in the SAME order in which you recorded them above) in the boxes below.

9	7	9	3

 21

MYSTERY WORD

After reading about the **White House**, determine if each statement below is true or false. Color or shade the boxes of the **TRUE** statements. Next, unscramble the mystery word using the large letters of the **TRUE** statements.

The president's helicopter is known as Air Force One. **A**	The White House was designed by an architect named Frédéric Auguste Bartholdi. **T**	The Situation Room is used for crisis management and military operations. **D**	The White House has two hundred twenty-two rooms. **F**
The White House has three elevators. **I**	Ronald Reagan had electricity added to the house for the first time. **O**	Jimmy Carter served as president from 1997-2001. **H**	President John Quincy Adams added the South and North Porticoes. **E**
In 1814, British troops set fire to multiple government buildings. **E**	The East Wing contains the offices of the First Lady. **R**	Washington oversaw the construction but never lived in the White House. **C**	The White House is located at 1600 Pennsylvania Avenue. **N**
The Oval Office is located in the West Wing. **E**	The South Lawn is where the president often arrives by helicopter. **S**	The Oval Office was built in 1902 during McKinley's presidency. **P**	The White House sits on forty acres of landscaped grounds. **L**

Unscramble the word using the large bold letters of only the **TRUE** statements.

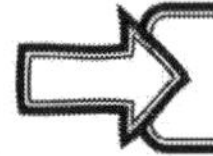

RESIDENCE

 22

PRESIDENT'S CABINET

MYSTERY MATCH

After reading about the **President's Cabinet**, draw a line from the left-hand column to make a match in the right-hand column. Your line should go through **ONE** letter. When you complete all the matches, use the letters with a line THROUGH them to unscramble a mystery word. You MUST start and end your line at the **arrow points**.

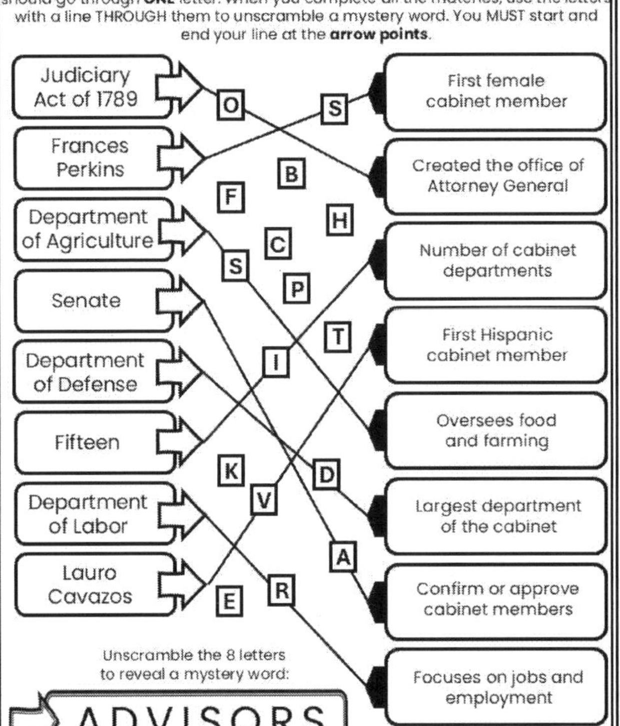

Unscramble the 8 letters to reveal a mystery word:

ADVISORS

MULTIPLE CHOICE

After reading about the **President's Cabinet**, answer each multiple-choice question below. Then, count the number of times you used each letter as an answer (ABCD) to reveal a 4-digit code. Letters may be used more than once or not at all. If a letter option is not used, put a zero in that box.

1 What department handles international relationships with other countries?
A. Department of State
B. Department of Exterior
C. Department of Interior
D. Department of Commerce

2 Norman Mineta became the first Asian American cabinet member to serve in what role?
A. Secretary of Education
B. Secretary of Commerce
C. Attorney General
D. Secretary of State

3 Which department works on promoting the economy?
A. Commerce
B. Treasury
C. Labor
D. Interior

4 Who was the first Black American to serve as Secretary of State?
A. Colin Powell
B. Frances Perkins
C. Robert Weaver
D. Norman Mineta

5 Who was Washington's Secretary of War?
A. Henry Knox
B. Alexander Hamilton
C. Thomas Jefferson
D. Frances Perkins

6 Which department works to prevent terrorism?
A. Housing and Urban Development
B. Homeland Security
C. Commerce
D. Labor

7 Who first described the meetings of his advisors as the "president's cabinet"?
A. George Washington
B. Thomas Jefferson
C. John Adams
D. James Madison

8 Which department head has the title of Attorney General?
A. Justice
B. Labor
C. Education
D. Homeland Security

Count how many times you used each letter as a correct answer (ABCD) to determine the 4-digit code. Record your answer in the boxes below.

# of A's	# of B's	# of C's	# of D's
5	2	0	1

 24

PRESIDENTIAL ELECTIONS

TRUE OR FALSE

After reading about **Presidential Elections**, read each statement below and determine if it is true or false. If the statement is true, color the coin that corresponds with that question. If the statement is false, cross out that coin value. When you are finished, add the TOTAL of **ALL TRUE** coin values to reveal a 4-digit code. One digit of the code has been provided for you. If the total is 625, a 6 would go in the first box, the 2 in the second box and so on.

A. The 18th Amendment of the Constitution outlines presidential term limits.

B. A closed primary means that voters that do not belong to a party can vote.

C. Each political party has a committee which raises money for the campaign and TV commercials.

D. In some states, voters are automatically registered when they get a driver's license or state ID.

E. Election Day is held the first Tuesday after the first Monday in November.

F. There are 538 electors in the Electoral College.

G. Presidential candidates have to live in the U.S. for at least twenty years.

H. At national conventions, the presidential candidate chooses a running-mate or vice president.

Coins: A (crossed out), B (crossed out), C 50, D 100, E 100, F 75, G (crossed out), H 25

After shading the coins based on your answer, add the value of ALL TRUE statements to get the final total. Record your answer in the boxes below.

3	5	0	9

© Think Tank Teacher 25

DOUBLE PUZZLE

After reading about **Presidential Elections**, determine the word that corresponds with the statements provided below. Spell the corresponding word in the boxes to the right. You may or may not use all squares provided for each answer. Any numerical answers must be spelled out. Next, use the numbers **under** indicated letters to reveal a secret word.

#	Statement	Answer	Numbers under letters
1	The month Election Day occurs	NOVEMBER	N = 8, M = 3
2	Minimum number of electors in each state	THREE	
3	Minimum age to vote	EIGHTEEN	I = 6
4	Number of terms a president can serve	TWO	
5	There are two types of ___ elections: open and closed	PRIMARY	P = 4
6	Group of presidential advisors	CABINET	A = 2
7	Synonym for armed forces	MILITARY	A = 5
8	Some states hold ___ rather than primaries	CAUCUSES	C = 1
9	Number of presidential requirements outlined in the Constitution	THREE	
10	___ officially declared Election Day in 1845	CONGRESS	G = 7

SECRET WORD

C	A	M	P	A	I	G	N
1	2	3	4	5	6	7	8

© Think Tank Teacher 26

STATE OF THE UNION ADDRESS

PARAGRAPH CODE

After reading about the **State of the Union Address**, head back to the reading and number ALL the paragraphs in the reading passage. Then, read each statement below and determine which paragraph **NUMBER** the statement can be found in. Paragraph numbers MAY be used more than one time or not at all. Follow the directions below to reveal the 4-digit code.

A The tradition of having a designated survivor gained prominence during the Cold War era when concerns about nuclear attacks were high. **12**

B The average speech lasts one hour, although Richard Nixon's 1972 State of the Union speech lasted just twenty-eight minutes. **3**

C Back then, the speech was called the "Annual Message" because the president would present his message to Congress. **6**

D Each year, the State of the Union Address typically takes place in late January or early February. **1**

E A designated survivor is a high-ranking government official who is chosen to remain in a secure and undisclosed location during the Address. **14**

F Calvin Coolidge, America's 30th president, made history with his State of the Union Address in 1923. **9**

G In 1913, President Woodrow Wilson gave the speech in person to create support of the president's agenda. **8**

H Jefferson believed that delivering the address in person resembled the British monarch's "Speech from the Throne." **7**

ELIMINATE ALL EVEN-NUMBERED paragraphs that you used as an answer. Record the remaining numbers (in the SAME order in which you recorded them above) in the boxes below.

3	1	9	7

© Think Tank Teacher 27

MYSTERY WORD

After reading about the **State of the Union Address**, determine if each statement below is true or false. Color or shade the boxes of the **TRUE** statements. Next, unscramble the mystery word using the large letters of the **TRUE** statements.

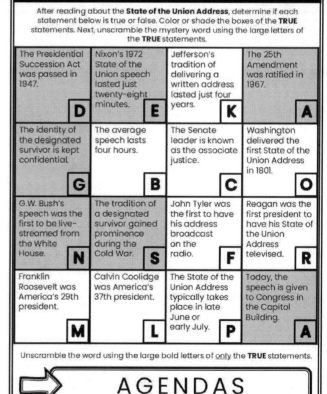

The Presidential Succession Act was passed in 1947. **D** (shaded)	Nixon's 1972 State of the Union speech lasted just twenty-eight minutes. **E** (shaded)	Jefferson's tradition of delivering a written address lasted just four years. **K**	The 25th Amendment was ratified in 1967. **A** (shaded)
The identity of the designated survivor is kept confidential. **G** (shaded)	The average speech lasts four hours. **B**	The Senate leader is known as the associate justice. **C**	Washington delivered the first State of the Union Address in 1801. **O**
G.W. Bush's speech was the first to be live-streamed from the White House. **N** (shaded)	The tradition of a designated survivor gained prominence during the Cold War. **S** (shaded)	John Tyler was the first to have his address broadcast on the radio. **F**	Reagan was the first president to have his State of the Union Address televised. **R**
Franklin Roosevelt was America's 29th president. **M**	Calvin Coolidge was America's 37th president. **L**	The State of the Union Address typically takes place in late June or early July. **P**	Today, the speech is given to Congress in the Capitol Building. **A** (shaded)

Unscramble the word using the large bold letters of only the **TRUE** statements.

AGENDAS

© Think Tank Teacher 28

ELECTORAL COLLEGE

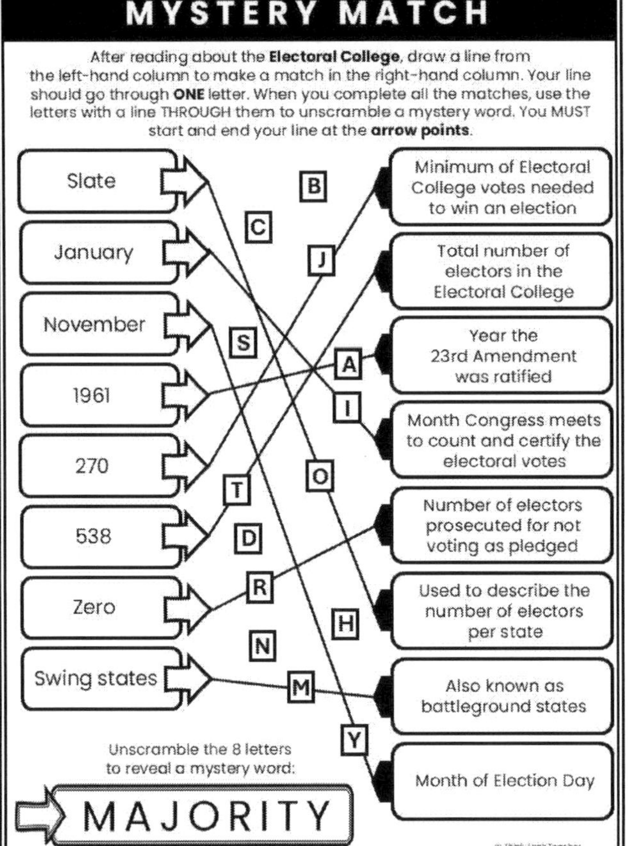

MYSTERY MATCH

After reading about the **Electoral College**, draw a line from the left-hand column to make a match in the right-hand column. Your line should go through **ONE** letter. When you complete all the matches, use the letters with a line THROUGH them to unscramble a mystery word. You MUST start and end your line at the **arrow points**.

Slate	B	Minimum of Electoral College votes needed to win an election
January	C	Total number of electors in the Electoral College
November	J	Year the 23rd Amendment was ratified
1961	S	Month Congress meets to count and certify the electoral votes
270	A	Number of electors prosecuted for not voting as pledged
538	I	Used to describe the number of electors per state
Zero	O	Also known as battleground states
Swing states	T	Month of Election Day
	D	
	R	
	H	
	N	
	M	
	Y	

Unscramble the 8 letters to reveal a mystery word:

MAJORITY

© Think Tank Teacher

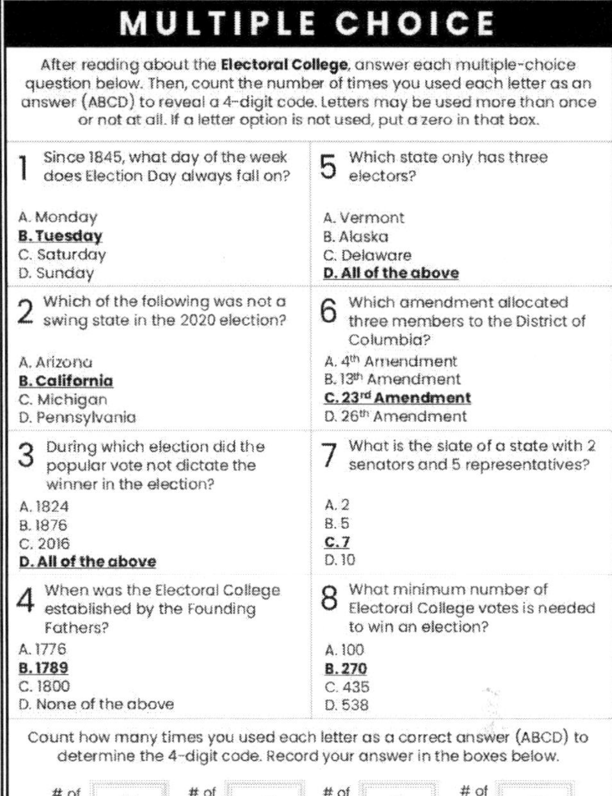

MULTIPLE CHOICE

After reading about the **Electoral College**, answer each multiple-choice question below. Then, count the number of times you used each letter as an answer (ABCD) to reveal a 4-digit code. Letters may be used more than once or not at all. If a letter option is not used, put a zero in that box.

1 Since 1845, what day of the week does Election Day always fall on?
A. Monday
B. Tuesday
C. Saturday
D. Sunday

2 Which of the following was not a swing state in the 2020 election?
A. Arizona
B. California
C. Michigan
D. Pennsylvania

3 During which election did the popular vote not dictate the winner in the election?
A. 1824
B. 1876
C. 2016
D. All of the above

4 When was the Electoral College established by the Founding Fathers?
A. 1776
B. 1789
C. 1800
D. None of the above

5 Which state only has three electors?
A. Vermont
B. Alaska
C. Delaware
D. All of the above

6 Which amendment allocated three members to the District of Columbia?
A. 4th Amendment
B. 13th Amendment
C. 23rd Amendment
D. 26th Amendment

7 What is the slate of a state with 2 senators and 5 representatives?
A. 2
B. 5
C. 7
D. 10

8 What minimum number of Electoral College votes is needed to win an election?
A. 100
B. 270
C. 435
D. 538

Count how many times you used each letter as a correct answer (ABCD) to determine the 4-digit code. Record your answer in the boxes below.

# of A's	# of B's	# of C's	# of D's
0	4	2	2

© Think Tank Teacher 30

POLITICAL PARTIES

TRUE OR FALSE

After reading about **Political Parties**, read each statement below and determine if it is true or false. If the statement is true, color the coin that corresponds with that question. If the statement is false, cross out that coin value. When you are finished, add the TOTAL of **ALL TRUE** coin values to reveal a 4-digit code. One digit of the code has been provided for you. If the total is 625, a 6 would go in the first box, the 2 in the second box and so on.

A. The Federalist Party was led by James Madison.

B. Republicans emphasize limited government, free-market capitalism, lower taxes, and individual responsibility.

C. The basic disagreement among Democrats and Republicans is the role of the government.

D. In 1861, Abraham Lincoln became the first Democratic president.

E. The Republican Party symbol is the elephant.

F. In 1834, the Whig Party formed in response to Jackson's view of the National Bank.

G. Democrats are often referred to as "conservatives."

H. A political party is a group of people who share the same political beliefs.

Coins: A (crossed out) · E 100 · B 25 · F 75 · C 50 · G (crossed out) · D (crossed out) · H 25

After shading the coins based on your answer, add the value of ALL TRUE statements to get the final total. Record your answer in the boxes below.

2	7	5	3

© Think Tank Teacher 31

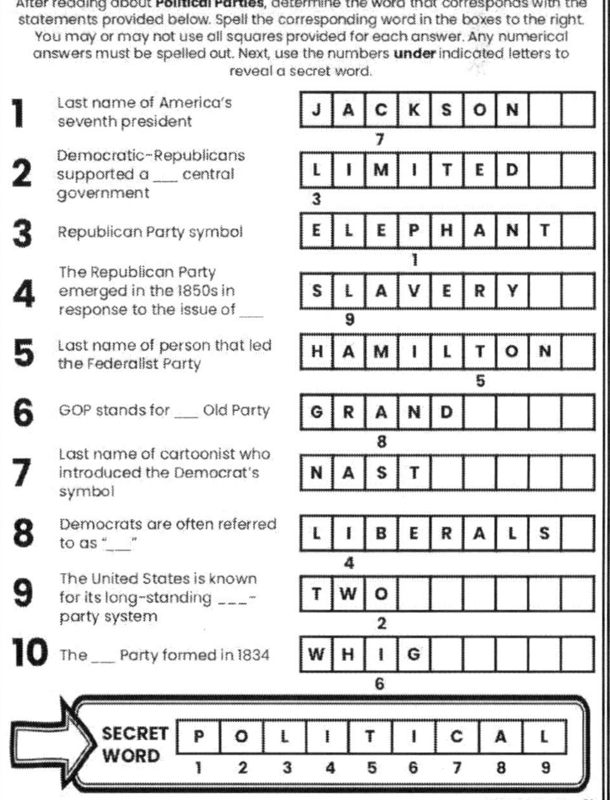

DOUBLE PUZZLE

After reading about **Political Parties**, determine the word that corresponds with the statements provided below. Spell the corresponding word in the boxes to the right. You may or may not use all squares provided for each answer. Any numerical answers must be spelled out. Next, use the numbers **under** indicated letters to reveal a secret word.

1 Last name of America's seventh president — J A C K S O N (7)

2 Democratic-Republicans supported a ___ central government — L I M I T E D (3)

3 Republican Party symbol — E L E P H A N T (1)

4 The Republican Party emerged in the 1850s in response to the issue of ___ — S L A V E R Y (9)

5 Last name of person that led the Federalist Party — H A M I L T O N (5)

6 GOP stands for ___ Old Party — G R A N D (8)

7 Last name of cartoonist who introduced the Democrat's symbol — N A S T

8 Democrats are often referred to as "___" — L I B E R A L S (4)

9 The United States is known for its long-standing ___-party system — T W O (2)

10 The ___ Party formed in 1834 — W H I G (6)

SECRET WORD

P	O	L	I	T	I	C	A	L
1	2	3	4	5	6	7	8	9

© Think Tank Teacher 32

JUDICIAL BRANCH

PARAGRAPH CODE

After reading about the **Judicial Branch**, head back to the reading and number ALL the paragraphs in the reading passage. Then, read each statement below and determine which paragraph **NUMBER** the statement can be found in. Paragraph numbers MAY be used more than one time or not at all. Follow the directions below to reveal the 4-digit code.

A These courts consist of three judges but there is no jury, no witnesses and no new evidence is presented. **4**

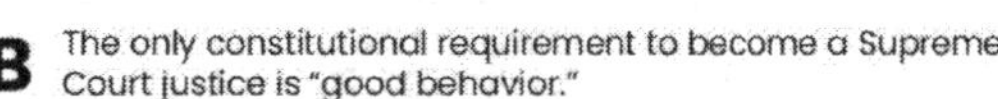

B The only constitutional requirement to become a Supreme Court justice is "good behavior." **6**

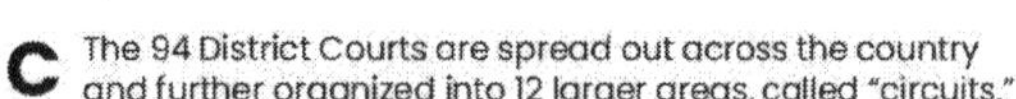

C The 94 District Courts are spread out across the country and further organized into 12 larger areas, called "circuits." **3**

D The court system in the Judicial Branch is structured in a hierarchy. **2**

E The only court listed in the U.S. Constitution is the Supreme Court, giving Congress the power to create lower courts. **8**

F The judicial process helps ensure that every person has a fair trial with an honest, competent (qualified) judge. **9**

G District Courts are trial courts where a judge and jury determine guilt or innocence. **3**

H The members of the Supreme Court are appointed, or chosen, by the president, then confirmed by the Senate. **5**

ELIMINATE ALL EVEN-NUMBERED paragraphs that you used as an answer. Record the remaining numbers (in the SAME order in which you recorded them above) in the boxes below.

3 9 3 5

MYSTERY WORD

After reading about the **Judicial Branch**, determine if each statement below is true or false. Color or shade the boxes of the **TRUE** statements. Next, unscramble the mystery word using the large letters of the **TRUE** statements.

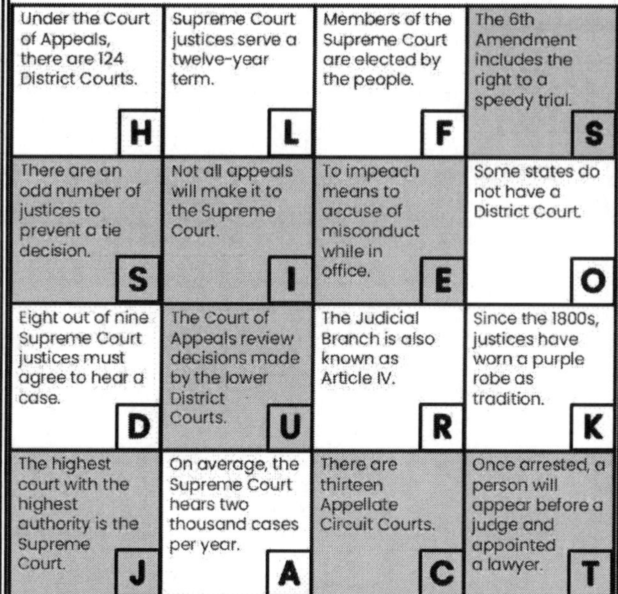

Under the Court of Appeals, there are 124 District Courts. H
Supreme Court justices serve a twelve-year term. L
Members of the Supreme Court are elected by the people. F
The 6th Amendment includes the right to a speedy trial. S
There are an odd number of justices to prevent a tie decision. S
Not all appeals will make it to the Supreme Court. I
To impeach means to accuse of misconduct while in office. E
Some states do not have a District Court. O
Eight out of nine Supreme Court justices must agree to hear a case. D
The Court of Appeals review decisions made by the lower District Courts. U
The Judicial Branch is also known as Article IV. R
Since the 1800s, justices have worn a purple robe as tradition. K
The highest court with the highest authority is the Supreme Court. J
On average, the Supreme Court hears two thousand cases per year. A
There are thirteen Appellate Circuit Courts. C
Once arrested, a person will appear before a judge and appointed a lawyer. T

Unscramble the word using the large bold letters of only the **TRUE** statements.

JUSTICES

SUPREME COURT

MYSTERY MATCH

After reading about the **Supreme Court**, draw a line from the left-hand column to make a match in the right-hand column. Your line should go through **ONE** letter. When you complete all the matches, use the letters with a line THROUGH them to unscramble a mystery word. You MUST start and end your line at the **arrow points.**

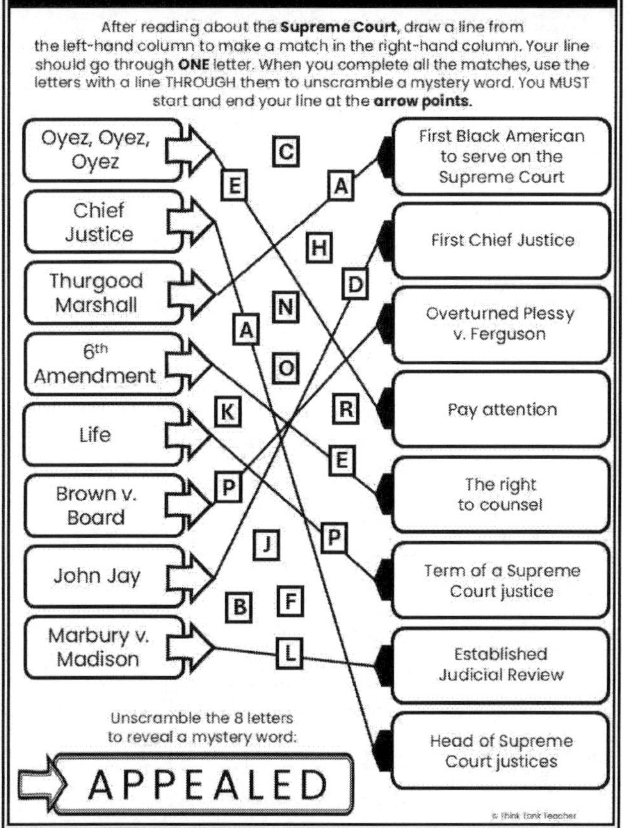

Unscramble the 8 letters to reveal a mystery word:

APPEALED

MULTIPLE CHOICE

After reading about the **Supreme Court**, answer each multiple-choice question below. Then, count the number of times you used each letter as an answer (ABCD) to reveal a 4-digit code. Letters may be used more than once or not at all. If a letter option is not used, put a zero in that box.

1 Justices can serve a life-term in the Supreme Court until which of the following?
A. Impeachment
B. Retirement
C. Death
D. All of the above

2 Who was the first woman to serve on the Supreme Court, appointed by President Ronald Reagan?
A. Sandra Day O'Connor
B. Sonia Sotomayor
C. Ruth Bader Ginsburg
D. None of the above

3 When the Supreme Court was first founded in 1789, what was it known as?
A. 14th Circuit Court
B. The President's Palace
C. The Nation's Court
D. Liberty Building

4 Who famously wore a dissent necklace to signal when she disagreed with the majority?
A. Sandra Day O'Connor
B. Sonia Sotomayor
C. Ruth Bader Ginsburg
D. None of the above

5 Which landmark case was about a person understanding their rights and self-incrimination?
A. Gideon v. Wainwright
B. Plessy v. Ferguson
C. Miranda v. Arizona
D. Tinker v. Des Moines

6 When did Marbury v. Madison establish Judicial Review?
A. 1789
B. 1793
C. 1801
D. 1803

7 Of nine justices, how many must agree to hear a case?
A. Four
B. Five
C. Six
D. Nine

8 When a justice disagrees with the decision of the majority, what opinion is given?
A. Majority opinion
B. Closed opinion
C. Dissenting opinion
D. Circuit opinion

Count how many times you used each letter as a correct answer (ABCD) to determine the 4-digit code. Record your answer in the boxes below.

# of A's	# of B's	# of C's	# of D's
2	0	4	2

LANDMARK CASES

TRUE OR FALSE

After reading about **Landmark Cases**, read each statement below and determine if it is true or false. If the statement is true, color the coin that corresponds with that question. If the statement is false, cross out that coin value. When you are finished, add the TOTAL of **ALL TRUE** coin values to reveal a 4-digit code. One digit of the code has been provided for you. If the total is 625, a 6 would go in the first box, the 2 in the second box and so on.

A. Mary Beth Tinker argued that a persons' right to legal counsel should not depend on whether they can afford one.

B. To interrogate means to ask questions.

C. Plessy argued that the state of Louisiana was in violation of the Equal Protection Clause of the 14th Amendment.

D. The Miranda case led to policy that is still practiced today.

E. The U.S. Supreme Court often deals with some of the most challenging legal issues facing the nation.

F. To protest the unpopular Korean War, the Tinkers wore green armbands to school.

G. The case of Gideon v Wainwright in 1963 was based on the First Amendment.

H. The Supreme Court ruled in favor of Miranda, claiming he was not properly informed of his constitutional rights.

Coins: A (crossed out), B 25, C 50, D 100, E 100, F (crossed out), G (crossed out), H 25

After shading the coins based on your answer, add the value of ALL TRUE statements to get the final total. Record your answer in the boxes below.

3	0	0	7

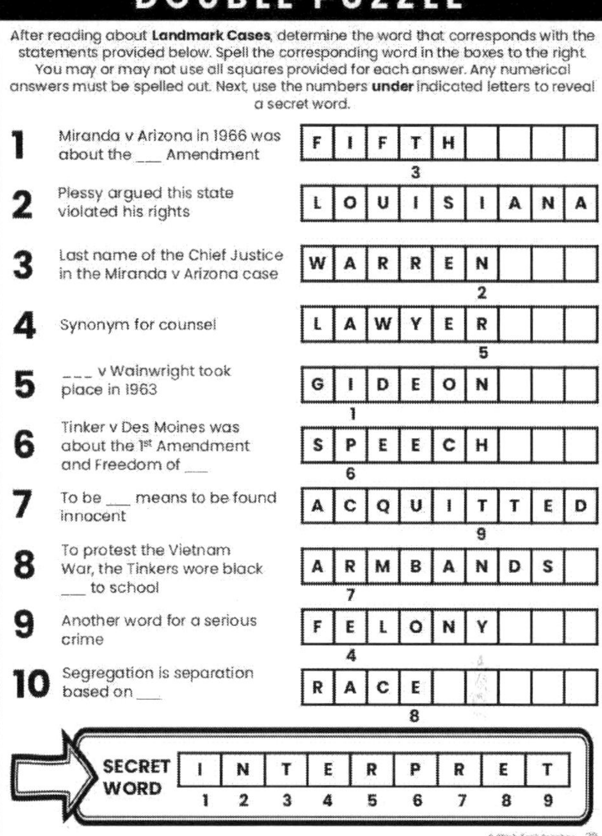

DOUBLE PUZZLE

After reading about **Landmark Cases**, determine the word that corresponds with the statements provided below. Spell the corresponding word in the boxes to the right. You may or may not use all squares provided for each answer. Any numerical answers must be spelled out. Next, use the numbers **under** indicated letters to reveal a secret word.

#	Statement	Answer	Number under letter
1	Miranda v Arizona in 1966 was about the ___ Amendment	FIFTH	3
2	Plessy argued this state violated his rights	LOUISIANA	
3	Last name of the Chief Justice in the Miranda v Arizona case	WARREN	2
4	Synonym for counsel	LAWYER	5
5	___ v Wainwright took place in 1963	GIDEON	1
6	Tinker v Des Moines was about the 1st Amendment and Freedom of ___	SPEECH	6
7	To be ___ means to be found innocent	ACQUITTED	9
8	To protest the Vietnam War, the Tinkers wore black ___ to school	ARMBANDS	7
9	Another word for a serious crime	FELONY	4
10	Segregation is separation based on ___	RACE	8

SECRET WORD

I	N	T	E	R	P	R	E	T
1	2	3	4	5	6	7	8	9

CRIMINAL V. CIVIL TRIALS

PARAGRAPH CODE

After reading about **Criminal v Civil Trials**, head back to the reading and number ALL the paragraphs in the reading passage. Then, read each statement below and determine which paragraph **NUMBER** the statement can be found in. Paragraph numbers MAY be used more than one time or not at all. Follow the directions below to reveal the 4-digit code.

	Statement	Paragraph
A	The role of a jury is not to determine guilt or innocence, rather to decide if there is enough evidence to prove a person is guilty of the crime.	12
B	The plaintiff, or victim, in a civil case usually sues for monetary "damages."	4
C	The outcome of civil cases does not result in the "losing" party serving jail time.	7
D	Probable cause can be found in the 4th Amendment of the U.S. Constitution.	9
E	The 8th Amendment prevents the judge from setting bail at one million dollars if the crime was stealing a candy bar.	10
F	Due process is the legal requirement that the government must respect all legal rights that are owed to a person.	2
G	Civil cases, or non-criminal cases, are a dispute between two or more parties.	3
H	A full trial may become unnecessary if a "motion for summary judgement" is filed during pre-trial.	5

ELIMINATE ALL EVEN-NUMBERED paragraphs that you used as an answer. Record the remaining numbers (in the SAME order in which you recorded them above) in the boxes below.

7	9	3	5

MYSTERY WORD

After reading about **Criminal v Civil Trials**, determine if each statement below is true or false. Color or shade the boxes of the **TRUE** statements. Next, unscramble the mystery word using the large letters of the **TRUE** statements.

Most juries in the United States have twelve members, called jurors. **D**	The defendant is presumed guilty until proven innocent. **M**	A composition is a formal interview or testimony. **A**	The 9th Amendment protects the right to a trial by jury in civil cases. **H**
Probable cause is "a reasonable belief that a crime has been committed." **N**	A civil case begins when a person files a complaint for at least $1000 dollars. **L**	Juries are optional for a civil case and many cases are decided solely by a judge. **E**	Probable cause can be found in the 12th Amendment. **G**
Laws of tort involve a person injured on someone else's property. **C**	The 6th Amendment gives citizens the right to legal counsel. **E**	If the verdict is guilty, sentencing takes place. **I**	About thirty percent of all civil cases happen at the state level. **R**
The plaintiff is the person or party whom the lawsuit has been filed against. **T**	There are four types of court cases: civil, parliamentary, open and closed. **P**	There are two main types of crimes: against people and against property. **E**	In a criminal trial, the case is always the Prosecutor v. Defendant. **V**

Unscramble the word using the large bold letters of only the **TRUE** statements.

EVIDENCE

THURGOOD MARSHALL

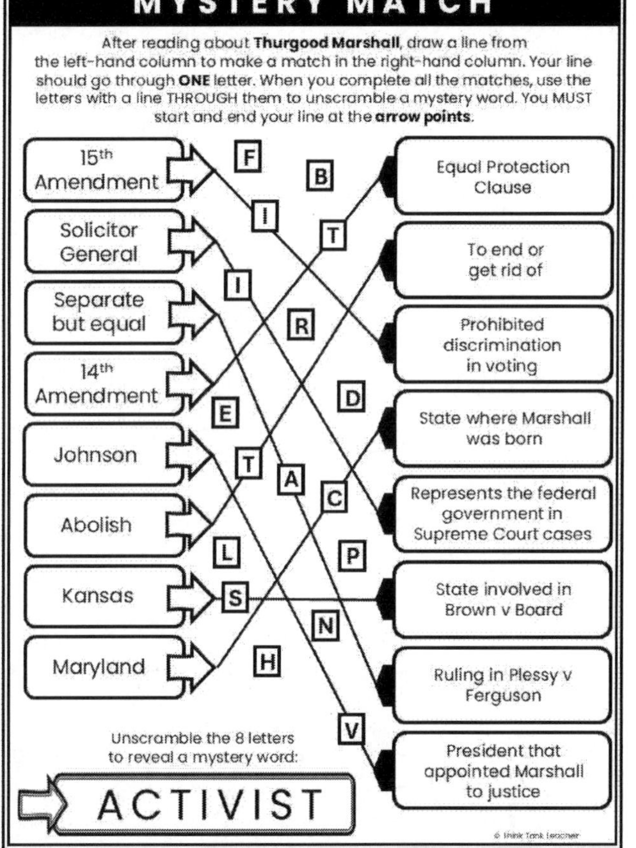

MYSTERY MATCH

After reading about **Thurgood Marshall**, draw a line from the left-hand column to make a match in the right-hand column. Your line should go through **ONE** letter. When you complete all the matches, use the letters with a line THROUGH them to unscramble a mystery word. You MUST start and end your line at the **arrow points**.

15th Amendment	Equal Protection Clause
Solicitor General	To end or get rid of
Separate but equal	Prohibited discrimination in voting
14th Amendment	State where Marshall was born
Johnson	Represents the federal government in Supreme Court cases
Abolish	State involved in Brown v Board
Kansas	Ruling in Plessy v Ferguson
Maryland	President that appointed Marshall to justice

F B I T I R D E T A C L P S N H V

Unscramble the 8 letters to reveal a mystery word:

ACTIVIST

© Think Tank Teacher

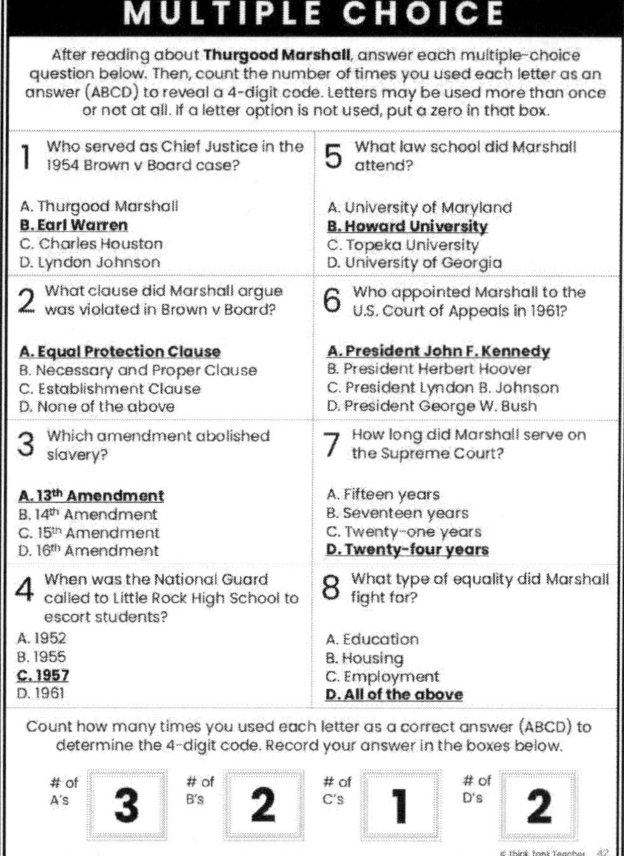

MULTIPLE CHOICE

After reading about **Thurgood Marshall**, answer each multiple-choice question below. Then, count the number of times you used each letter as an answer (ABCD) to reveal a 4-digit code. Letters may be used more than once or not at all. If a letter option is not used, put a zero in that box.

1 Who served as Chief Justice in the 1954 Brown v Board case?
A. Thurgood Marshall
B. Earl Warren
C. Charles Houston
D. Lyndon Johnson

2 What clause did Marshall argue was violated in Brown v Board?
A. Equal Protection Clause
B. Necessary and Proper Clause
C. Establishment Clause
D. None of the above

3 Which amendment abolished slavery?
A. 13th Amendment
B. 14th Amendment
C. 15th Amendment
D. 16th Amendment

4 When was the National Guard called to Little Rock High School to escort students?
A. 1952
B. 1955
C. 1957
D. 1961

5 What law school did Marshall attend?
A. University of Maryland
B. Howard University
C. Topeka University
D. University of Georgia

6 Who appointed Marshall to the U.S. Court of Appeals in 1961?
A. President John F. Kennedy
B. President Herbert Hoover
C. President Lyndon B. Johnson
D. President George W. Bush

7 How long did Marshall serve on the Supreme Court?
A. Fifteen years
B. Seventeen years
C. Twenty-one years
D. Twenty-four years

8 What type of equality did Marshall fight for?
A. Education
B. Housing
C. Employment
D. All of the above

Count how many times you used each letter as a correct answer (ABCD) to determine the 4-digit code. Record your answer in the boxes below.

# of A's	# of B's	# of C's	# of D's
3	2	1	2

© Think Tank Teacher 42

TINKER V DES MOINES

TRUE OR FALSE

After reading about **Tinker v Des Moines**, read each statement below and determine if it is true or false. If the statement is true, color the coin that corresponds with that question. If the statement is false, cross out that coin value. When you are finished, add the TOTAL of **ALL TRUE** coin values to reveal a 4-digit code. One digit of the code has been provided for you. If the total is 625, a 6 would go in the first box, the 2 in the second box and so on.

A. The District Court argued that the armbands could disrupt learning at school.
B. The First Amendment, adopted in 1776, includes seven freedoms.
C. In silent protest, the students wore black armbands anyway, with support from their parents.
D. Appeal means to ask a higher court to review the case.
E. The Supreme Court had to consider if free speech applied to symbolic speech.
F. The Tinker's won the case at the U.S. Court of Appeals for the Eighth Circuit.
G. In the 1960s, America was involved in the Vietnam War, which was an unpopular war with many.
H. Tinker v Des Moines was a landmark Supreme Court case from 1974 that addressed the Third Amendment.

Coins: A 75, E 100, B (X), F (X), C 50, G 50, D 100, H (X)

After shading the coins based on your answer, add the value of ALL TRUE statements to get the final total. Record your answer in the boxes below.

3	7	5	8

© Think Tank Teacher 43

DOUBLE PUZZLE

After reading about **Tinker v Des Moines**, determine the word that corresponds with the statements provided below. Spell the corresponding word in the boxes to the right. You may or may not use all squares provided for each answer. Any numerical answers must be spelled out. Next, use the numbers **under** indicated letters to reveal a secret word.

#	Clue	Answer	Number
1	Last name of the justice that delivered the majority opinion	F O R T A S	5 (under O)
2	In the 1960s, America was involved in the ___ War	V I E T N A M	3 (under M)
3	ACLU stands for American ___ Liberties Union	C I V I L	8 (under C)
4	Color of the armbands that students wore in protest	B L A C K	4 (under B)
5	___ B. Johnson served as America's thirty-sixth president	L Y N D O N	2 (under Y)
6	The 14th Amendment includes the "Due Process" and "___ Protection" clauses	E Q U A L	6 (under L)
7	Last name of the Tinker's attorney	J O H N S T O N	1 (under S)
8	Certiorari is reexamination of an action of a ___ court	L O W E R	
9	The state where Des Moines is located	I O W A	
10	Number of freedoms included in the First Amendment	F I V E	7 (under I)

SECRET WORD

S	Y	M	B	O	L	I	C
1	2	3	4	5	6	7	8

© Think Tank Teacher 44

MIRANDA V ARIZONA

PARAGRAPH CODE

After reading about **Miranda v Arizona**, head back to the reading and number ALL the paragraphs in the reading passage. Then, read each statement below and determine which paragraph **NUMBER** the statement can be found in. Paragraph numbers MAY be used more than one time or not at all. Follow the directions below to reveal the 4-digit code.

	Statement	#
A	Law enforcement can ask questions related to immediate public safety without reading the Miranda Rights.	6
B	The 5th and 6th Amendments were added to the Bill of Rights on December 15, 1791.	4
C	The landmark Supreme Court case, Miranda v. Arizona (1966), fundamentally changed how law enforcement interacts with suspects in custody.	1
D	The Fifth Amendment states that no person "shall be compelled in any criminal case to be a witness against himself."	5
E	Miranda's defense attorneys argued that his confession was unconstitutional because he had not been informed of his rights prior to the interrogation.	3
F	The police had little direct evidence linking Miranda to the crime but had suspicions based on circumstantial evidence.	2
G	In a 5-4 decision, the Supreme Court ruled in Miranda's favor.	8
H	The case was eventually appealed to the United States Supreme Court.	7

ELIMINATE ALL EVEN-NUMBERED paragraphs that you used as an answer. Record the remaining numbers (in the SAME order in which you recorded them above) in the boxes below.

1	5	3	7

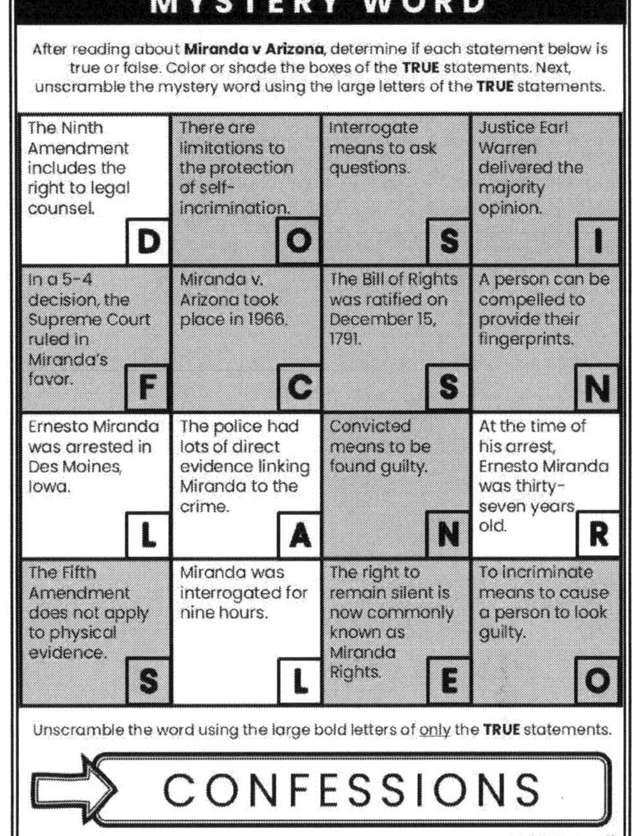

MYSTERY WORD

After reading about **Miranda v Arizona**, determine if each statement below is true or false. Color or shade the boxes of the **TRUE** statements. Next, unscramble the mystery word using the large letters of the **TRUE** statements.

The Ninth Amendment includes the right to legal counsel. **D**	There are limitations to the protection of self-incrimination. **O**	Interrogate means to ask questions. **S**	Justice Earl Warren delivered the majority opinion. **I**
In a 5-4 decision, the Supreme Court ruled in Miranda's favor. **F**	Miranda v. Arizona took place in 1966. **C**	The Bill of Rights was ratified on December 15, 1791. **S**	A person can be compelled to provide their fingerprints. **N**
Ernesto Miranda was arrested in Des Moines, Iowa. **L**	The police had lots of direct evidence linking Miranda to the crime. **A**	Convicted means to be found guilty. **N**	At the time of his arrest, Ernesto Miranda was thirty-seven years old. **R**
The Fifth Amendment does not apply to physical evidence. **S**	Miranda was interrogated for nine hours. **L**	The right to remain silent is now commonly known as Miranda Rights. **E**	To incriminate means to cause a person to look guilty. **O**

Unscramble the word using the large bold letters of only the **TRUE** statements.

CONFESSIONS

TERMS OF USE

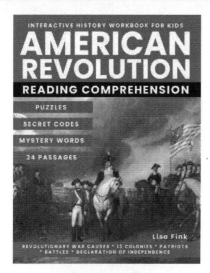

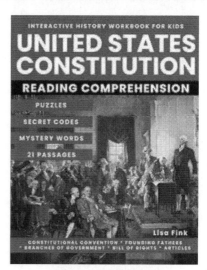